Hamlet's Wounded Name

by

Haldeen Braddy

Second enlarged edition

Preface by
James T. Bratcher

RODOPI N.V.

AMSTERDAM 1974

© Editions Rodopi N.V., Amsterdam
Library of Congress Card Number 74–76957
ISBN: 90–6203–018–1

TABLE OF CONTENTS

A FOREGLIMPSE AT HAMLET THE TRICKSTER

James T. Bratcher

The "Mouse-trap" of Act III mirrors much of the matter of *Hamlet,* and of this, the playlet, the Prince acts as stage-manager. Professor Braddy prompts us to recognize his role as stage-manager throughout the play and not merely with regard to the "trap," the pretended "ecstasy," the outmaneuvering of Rosencrantz and Guildenstern, and other ploys. This he urges despite the irresolution of the soliloquies, of which more later. A creature of Oedipal fixation? Decidedly not. Hamlet remains as dramatically human in his reaction to his father's murderer occupying his father's throne and bed as circumstances permit. (This is revenge tragedy, and of an acutely aggravated sort. Avengers *should* be disturbed.) A sequestered student incapable of action? Again, "No." Although he undergoes transformation, Hamlet does not procrastinate as a namby-pamby but makes haste deliberately, his considered aim being to ferret the full extent of the "something rotten," to determine mainly the Queen's and Ophelia's culpability while allowing Claudius to sweat in the protracted uncertainty that his crime deserves. On this view, the Ghost-admonished Prince *steadily* contrives to flush his birds one at a time; to manipulate the court; to disrupt plans in motion so as to avenge those realized. His apparent wavering explains itself partly in terms of his disarming tactics, partly as a natural concomitant of his "fact-finding mission," to use the modern cliché — a hesitancy reflecting, as Braddy says, "his inability to reconstruct and assimilate at once all of the pre-play political machinations that occurred during his absence from the Danish court."

To do his detective's work Hamlet simulates madness. His masquerade in the manner of Saxo's Amleth — a point of emphasis in Braddy's study, but not therein elaborated from one special viewpoint — forms the subject of this brief note. In a meaningful way *Hamlet* as the refined descendant of Danish legend partakes of a genre which Karl Kerényi, in other connections, has labeled "picaresque mythology," the literature of tricksters.[1] Appreciation of this neglected fact could help

Author of a number of papers on literary and folklore topics, James T. Bratcher has co-edited (with Lyle H. Kendall, Jr.) *A Suppressed Critique of Wise's Swinburne Transactions* (Austin: Humanities Research Center of the University of Texas, 1970) and recently has published *Analytical Index to Publications of the Texas Folklore Society, Volumes 1-36* (Dallas: Southern Methodist University Press, 1973).

toward explaining certain effects of the play otherwise puzzling in their insistence on contradictions, disorder, ebb and flow — the ineffable coming-apart that "steady" Hamlet experiences in his course.

Mythologists and folklorists recognize an archetypal figure sometimes known as Marplot. In some respects he is the Demiurge of Platonism; the character Unferth ("mar-peace") of *Beowulf* may represent an embodiment; most certainly do the Greek Hermes, the German Tyll Eulenspiegel, the African Spider Man, the American Indian Wakd-junkaga, the English Old Nick (Old Hob) and Lord of Misrule, and the Norse god Loki, to name but a few. (For Braddy's likening of Hamlet to Loki see pages 55, 62-63, 69.) Universally he is known as a trickster, or the Trickster, and he seems connected with ritual drama. Lord Raglan particularizes him by another name, *Spielman,* and it should serve to underscore Braddy's argument — for Hamlet approximates just such a one as here described — to quote Lord Raglan at length:[2]

> In Reinhardt's wonderful production *The Miracle,* the incidents of which are traditional and clearly derived from ritual drama, there is a character called the "Spielman." He appears in a different guise in each act, but it is he who initiates each dramatic development and who goads the other characters into action. The action ... always leads to their own ruin, but without his stimulation it does not appear that there would be any action at all. His role, though ostensibly that of a minor character, is really that of a prompter and stage-manager.
>
> In *Faust* we find a similar phenomenon. Here Mephistopheles, though he himself plays no part in the drama, is the motive-power behind the other characters ....
>
> [Mephistopheles' function] seems to have been foreshadowed in late pagan Scandinavia. "Among the gods," says Professor Gronbech [*The Culture of the Teutons*], "Loki occupies a place of his own. His part in the sacred drama is that of the plotter who sets the conflict in motion .... As the wily father of artifice whose office is to drag the demoniacal powers into the play and effect their downfall, he comes very near representing evil ...."
>
> ... In the Arthurian legend the Spielman is Merlin, who is always turning up in unexpected guises and urging the other characters on to deeds, usually of violence.
>
> The Homeric poems are of composite origin, and in the *Iliad* there is no regular Spielman, though Zeus occasionally takes the part. In the *Odyssey,* on the other hand, the part is taken regularly by Athena, that is, presumably by the priestess who represents her. She makes the spears of the suitors ineffective;

she strikes the suitors with panic; she causes Dawn to wake Odysseus; she infuses fresh vigour into Laertes; she consults with Zeus (presumably the presiding priest) as to the future course of events. "It is obvious," says Miss Stawell [F.M. Stawell: *Homer and the Iliad*], "that we cannot think of her in this case as an all-wise prophetess, for . . . she is urging her favourite on a course she knows will end in bitterest grief."

. . . It seems probable that in the earliest ritual drama, in Greece and elsewhere, the Spielman spoke but did not act, and the other characters acted but did not speak.

Lord Raglan's paragraphs suggest Hamlet's affinity with a character-type who (however) prefigures him only half way. Except for the dumb show and playlet that he arranges, Hamlet, although answering in other respects, does not dispose the elements of ruin chiefly from the wings or backstage, much less from Olympus or the nether region. But if anything, his center-stage show of artifice and grim clownishness the more so invites notice from the standpoint of picaresque mythology. T. S. Eliot in his famous essay, "Hamlet and His Problems," has regarded Hamlet's equivocal behavior as "less than madness and more than feigned." Hamlet's demon, Eliot states, remains inexplicable to him and to us. "The intense feeling, ecstatic or terrible, without an object or exceeding its object, is something which every person of sensibility has known; it is doubtless a subject of study for pathologists."

Now, pathologists have indeed studied the phenomenon, and in connection with the Trickster. Jung in his commentary appended to Paul Radin's *The Trickster: A Study in American Indian Mythology* (New York: Philosophical Library, 1956) has recourse to the archetype which he names the *shadow* and which consists in civilized man's vestigial remembrance of his bestial origin. "Taking it in its deepest sense, the shadow is the invisible saurian tail that man still drags behind him."[3] One of its most common embodiments is the devil, representing "the dangerous aspect of the unrecognized dark half of the personality."[4] In the commentary referred to, Jung writes of the shadow as externalized also in the Trickster:

In picaresque tales, in carnivals and revels, in sacred and magical rites, in man's religious fears and exaltations, this phantom of the trickster haunts the mythology of all ages, sometimes in quite unmistakable form, sometimes in strangely modulated guise. He is obviously a 'psychologem,' an archetypal psychic structure of extreme antiquity. In his clearest manifestations he is a faithful copy of the absolutely undifferentiated human consciousness, corresponding to a psyche that has hardly left the animal level . . . .

> ... In many cultures his figure seems like an old river-bed in which the water still flows. One can see this best of all from the fact that the trickster motif does not crop up only in its original form but appears just as naively and authentically in the unsuspecting modern man — whenever, in fact, he feels himself at the mercy of annoying 'accidents' which thwart his will and his actions with apparently malicious intent. He then speaks of 'hoodoos' and 'ginxes' or of the 'mischieviousness of the object' . . . .[5]
>
> ... The so-called civilized man ... remembers [the trickster] only figuratively and metaphorically, when, irritated by his own ineptitude, he speaks of fate playing tricks on him or of things being bewitched. He never suspects that his own hidden and apparently harmless shadow has qualities whose dangerousness exceeds his wildest dreams. As soon as people get together in masses and submerge the individual, the shadow is mobilized, and, as history shows, may even be personified and incarnated.[6]

With ample reason, one may argue that the shadow is "mobilized" in *Hamlet*; that the Prince's condition, "less than madness and more than feigned," results from precisely this demon — the "saurian" Trickster within the trickster, struggling to assert itself once conjured in a civilized being; that the returned sea voyager's cynicism and remorselessness concerning Rosencrantz and Guildenstern bespeak a giving way to the "dangerous aspect" of this "dark half" within him. Braddy rightly characterizes Hamlet's mood in informing Horatio of the death of the witless and innocent courtiers as one of "stern exultation," signaling, as he says, Hamlet's thorough transformation as the "avenger incarnate." He cites this passage, remarkable for its suggestion of the emerged Machiavel triumphant in the sensitive moralist:

> Why, man, they did make love to this employment.
> They are not near my conscience; their defeat
> Does by their own insinuation grow:
> 'T is dangerous when the baser nature comes
> Between the pass and fell incensed points
> Of mighty opposites.

"Why, what a King is this! " exclaims Horatio, astounded by the change.

Braddy's final chapter, "Points of Mighty Opposites," examines Hamlet's no-longer-disguised opposition to Claudius in Act V. In developing his thesis of a hardened nemesis Braddy calls attention to the unusual recurrence of structural, stylistic, and thematic "opposites" in the play: the alternation of serious and comic scenes, the extravagant use of oxymoron, the pretended madness of Hamlet in contrast to Ophelia's actual derangement, and so on (pages 59-60). Collectively these tensions create the impression of a topsy-turvy world such as student Hamlet discovers at Elsinore; they function as a means to empathy. But not surprisingly, the topsy-turviness finds also a basis in picaresque mythology, so that possibly some deeper dramatic purpose is served. Both Kerényi and Jung approach this mythology as *par excellence* one of inversion and catharsis; Kerényi notes that it serves therapeutically to permit the experience of disorder in normally circumscribed human conduct,[7] and in the same vein Jung cites medieval religious observances (and of course *Mardi gras* remains nominally a religious observance) like the election of the Boy Bishop, the Feast of Fools, and the Ass Festival (in which congregations merrily knelt and brayed in semblance of the animal's homage to the Christ child) as healthily restoring the "older level of consciousness."[8] Jung, especially, considers picaresque mythology as satisfying "the polaristic structure of the psyche, which like any other energic system is dependent on the tension of opposites."[9] He concludes his commentary with the sentence: "As in its collective, mythological form, so also [does] the individual shadow [contain] within it the seed of an enantiodromia, of a conversion into its opposite."[10] Braddy likewise — it is interesting to note — introduces the Law of Polarity in discussing Hamlet and his drama (pages 60-61, 63). He writes, for example:

> The hero of the first Acts transforms himself into his opposite in the closing ones. At first he comes upon the stage pale from cloistered study, meditative, given to introspection in the soliloquies . . . . At the end he is weather-beaten from the sea, dueling confidently with Laertes, resolved that Denmark shall have a sovereign worthy of its destiny. It is significant that only in Act V does Hamlet forego his ubiquitous soliloquies . . . .

Could it be, then, that in terms of psychodrama the soliloquies have occurred therapeutically as restoring the "real" Hamlet (civilized man of intellect) as a necessary condition of his equilibrium as an effective trickster (primitive blood-avenger)? As Braddy observes, the soliloquies leave off by Act V; that is, by the time the "dark half" of Hamlet the Trickster has asserted itself fully.[11]

REFERENCES

1. "The Trickster in Relation to Greek Mythology," trans. R. F. C. Hull, in Radin (cited in the text), p. 175.

2. *The Hero: A Study in Tradition, Myth and Drama* (New York: Vintage, 1956), pp. 274-76.

3. *Psychological Reflections* (New York: Harper Torchbooks, 1961), p. 217.

4. *Essays on Analytical Psychology* (New York: Pantheon, 1953), p. 94.

5. "On the Psychology of the Trickster Figure," trans. R. F. C. Hull, in Radin, *op. cit.*, pp. 201-202.

6. *Ibid.*, p. 206.

7. "The Trickster in Relation to Greek Mythology," p. 185.

8. On the Psychology of the Trickster Figure," pp. 197-99.

9. *Ibid.*, p. 209.

10. *Ibid.*, p. 211.

11. Perhaps K. R. Eissler's *Discourse on Hamlet and "Hamlet"* (New York: International Universities Press, 1971) represents the most recent psychoanalytical approach to the play: here a Freudian treatment.

CLAUDIUS THE RAT AND HAMLET
THE TRICKSTER

Haldeen Braddy

In the remarkable rodent lore in *Hamlet,* the imagery of the Prince's uncle, Claudius, as a rat is the focus.[1] One aspect of animal parallelism introduced in the play may be studied in brief detail in order to exhibit the different levels of Shakespeare's meanings.

One of the chief components requiring more discussion consists of the folk element in Shakespeare's imagery, general as well as specific. In *Hamlet,* specifically, the epithet *rat* for Claudius matches the term *mouse* for *Gertrude.* Such rustic equation of the two murine farm denizens is a commonplace; the terms harmonize with Hamlet's reference to "country matters" (III, ii, 123). "Mouse" for the female embodies the image of the tinier, less repulsive, and more helpless — often a definitely eulogistic endearment. "Rat" for the male focuses on the fulsome image: larger, more loathesome, and more aggressive. Nonetheless, "rat"-"mouse" represents a male-female pairing of a certain known type.

The Prince anticipates that Claudius will call Gertrude "his mouse." In fact, Hamlet presumes that folkish word as a wifely endearment, even for a queen; in III, ii 240, Hamlet exacts of his mother that she refuse it henceforth. The imagery of the mouse pervades the play from the outset: in I, 1, 10, the query "Have you had quiet guard? " has for its answer, "Not a mouse stirring." The obvious proverbial report of perfect quiet would have an overlay in such a lusty play as this. The mice that would play and distract Danish soldiers on guard — women! Camp followers, in a word.

"The Mouse-trap" of Act III is set for the "mouse," to catch her; it is not baited with the "mouse" to capture the "rat." In point of fact, Hamlet devotes himself to observing and eliciting his mother's — the mouse's — reactions to his playlet as the action develops.

Hamlet must trap the mouse — his mother — in moving against her husband. If she turns out innocent of complicity in the murder of the first Hamlet, Gertrude must help her son. At the very least, she can withdraw her support from Claudius the usurper; then his brother's avenger can move less covertly. Or, preferably, the hapless Queen can actively, if discreetly, cooperate with her son in his scheme of retribution (as she does).

Hamlet's approach to his mother involves a still more sophisticated extension of mouse imagery. His mother is a namesake of the saint of

Nivelles, daughter of a king, who is associated with rats and field mice. St. Gertrude is characteristically portrayed as an abbess with these rodents at her feet, as I am informed by my former student, James Caroline. So much for Gertrude the Mouse.

With Claudius the Rat, a parallel turns up in Belleforest, whose *Histoires tragiques* is a known source of Shakespeare's play. The French author's "Roy Popiel mangé des rats" (*La Cosmographie universelle*) introduces the idea of a king whose name is associated with rats. My friend Witold Chwalewik has brought this point out in his article, "The Legend of King Popiel, A Possible Polish Source of 'Hamlett.' "[2] The phrase, "this is miching mallecho" (III, ii, 147), is cited by Chwalewik in the Q2 reading "munching Mallico" as a significant match of "mangé des rats" in Belleforest.[3]

Rather than "mangé des rats," King Claudius himself gnaws away like a rat, the idea conveyed by this imagery being that Hamlet's father was destroyed by a rat – or a mouse and a rat. The Queen Mouse, whom I hold innocent of killing Hamlet the Elder in the sense of "eating" him, is of course Gertrude.[4] The King Rat of this drama befouls its air, leading Marcellus to observe that "Something is rotten in the state of Denmark" (I, iv, 90). Claudius bulks in the foreground as veritable rodent – cunning, vicious, foul. The homely murine metaphor permeates the five acts of Shakespeare's play.

The animalian figure-of-speech in Act III reaches its climax in the titling of the playlet, "The Mouse-Trap." The avenging Prince has ended Act II by telling the audience that the play's the thing whereby he will catch the King's conscience.[5] That the King's nephew actually plans to work on the Queen's conscience, instead, figures as a dominant theme in my 1964 monograph, *Hamlet's Wounded Name*.[6] The apparent paradox of this approach underlines another dominant theme, that of Hamlet as the Scandinavian trickster figure, an interpretation developed in the last pages of my work.

In the *Shakespeare Quarterly* review of *Hamlet's Wounded Name*, "discovery of a new source in the Scandinavian trickster motif" is judged plausible enough. The reviewer's enlightened and favorable reception of my ideas then yields to sterner suspicion: "though very tenuous, so far as a definite analogue is concerned."[7] The reader may wonder too how the Danish lore of "Loki the *astucieux*" and of "Gunnlaug the Snake-tongued, lord of astringent speech"[8] would be known in Elizabethan England. In reply, one may point out that the archetype of a Scandinavian wily hero quite conceivably reached Shakespeare (writing around 1600) in a British issue of the *Gesta Danorum* of Saxo Grammaticus, published in 1514. In Saxo's Book VIII Loki, Norse god of mischief and intrigue, appears as Utgardilocus.[9]

Beyond the reasonable possibility of contact with Saxo's history, a more personal contact was readily open or available. English stage players visited the Danish court of Duke Charles at Nyköping during 1591 and 1592. Recent evidence of English activity in the theatre in Sweden and Finland about 1598-1600 bears directly on how Scandinavian culture and mythology came to the England of Elizabeth. The Danish King Frederick II had invited to his court in 1579 and to Elsinore in 1585 a troupe sponsored by the Duke of Leicester. Actors and musicians returned from these tours of Scandinavia presumably would bring back personal memories of Norse legend. Their accounts, it is postulated, would acquaint Shakespeare with the Danish Geste of Amleth and the locality of Elsinore. This circumstance would explain the Elizabethan playwright's transfer of the dramatic setting to Elsinore from Jutland (in the version of Saxo Grammaticus).[10]

The so-called sources of *Hamlet* do not involve line-by-line parallels. It is equally certain, however, that Shakespeare did not originate the idea of either the trickster Prince or rat King. The trickster prototype evidently came from Scandinavia, from the hearsay of Elizabethan actors or the printed pages of Saxo; the remarkable rodent image was plainly influenced by one of Shakespeare's favorite authors, Belleforest.

REFERENCES

1. George W. Williams, "The Complex Oedipus Complex," *Shakespeare Newsletter*, XVIII (April, 1968), 12.

2. Stanislaw Helaztynski, *Poland's Homage to Shakespeare* (Warsaw, Poland, 1965), p. 105.

3. *Ibid.*, p. 103.

4. For a further discussion of the play-within-the-play as a trap to catch the mouse, see my *Hamlet's Wounded Name* (El Paso, Texas, 1964), p. 28ff. A rat trap would of course catch a rat (Claudius), not a mouse (Gertrude). Hamlet thinks of his uncle as a rat and takes him for one (III, iv, 24).

5. *Ibid.*, p. 26.

6. *Ibid.*, pp. 19-28.

7. A. Louise Hastings (reviewer), *SQ*, XIX (1968), 186.

8. Braddy, *op. cit.*, p. 62.

9. Oliver Elton (tr.), *The First Nine Books of Danish History* (London, 1894), Book VIII, 352-57. The edition of 1514, now in the library of Texas Christian University, is discussed by Lyle H. Kendall, Jr., "Shakespeare Collections, Quartos, Source and Allusion Books in the W. L. Lewis Collection," *Shakespeare 1964* (Fort Worth, Texas, 1965), p. 166.

10. Erik Wikland, *Elizabethan Players in Sweden 1591-2: Facts and Problems* (Stockholm, 1962), pp. 5, 46, 92-94. See also Walter H. Blumenthal, *Paging Mr. Shakespeare* (New York, 1961), pp. 84, 261, 267.

A PROLOGUE, OR THE POSY

THE PRESENT MONOGRAPH, envisaged several years ago, was completed in 1964, the quadricentennial of Shakespeare's birth. An award as Research Professor of English for 1963-1964 from the Excellence Fund, Texas Western College, El Paso, made this study possible. Grateful acknowledgment is due the founder and administrator of the research program, President Joseph M. Ray. Similar acknowledgments go also to the Organized Research Fund, particularly for a grant to study in the Folger Shakespeare Library (Washington, D. C.) and for the services of an Assistant (Mr. Richard Escontrías); and to the Research Committee (Dr. John Sharp, Dean Ray Small, and Dean C. L. Sonnichsen) for examining both the preliminary outline of the project and the finished manuscript. Gratitude for various kinds of help is also due these former students: Mrs. Berenice Dittmer, Mr. Frank Feuille, Jr., Mr. Manuel Hornedo, Miss Karen Moore, and Miss Martha Piña, as well as several colleagues in the Department of English, especially Dr. Joseph L. Leach (Head), Dr. Robert Burlingame, Dr. A. S. Cairncross, Mrs. Lillian Collingwood, and Mrs. Eleanor Cotton Hall.

Particular thanks are tended Dr. S. D. Myres for stylistic suggestions and Mr. Carl Hertzog for the appropriate design of the book. The dedication to Dr. C. L. Sonnichsen is in recognition of his sincere interest in the project from its beginning.

— H. B.

El Paso, Texas
April, 1964

Hamlet's Wounded Name

BOOKS BY HALDEEN BRADDY

Three Chaucer Studies
(with others)

A Book of English Literature
(with others)

Reading Around the World
(with others)

Chaucer and the French Poet Graunson

Glorious Incense:
The Fulfillment of Edgar Allan Poe

Cock of the Walk:
The Legend of Pancho Villa

Hamlet's Wounded Name

Pershing's Mission in Mexico

Chaucer's Parlement of Foules

Pancho Villa Rides Again

Geoffrey Chaucer
Literary and Historical Studies

Mexico and the Old Southwest

Three Dimensional Poe

TO

CHARLES LELAND SONNICHSEN

Arrows and Slings

THE reputation of Shakespeare's Prince of Denmark, despite his many recent champions,[1] has been repeatedly belittled in the twentieth century. The trend in modern criticism to vindicate Rosencrantz and Guildenstern — Ophelia — Gertrude — even Claudius — has done much to dull the lustre of Hamlet's name.

In 1941 Dr. Samuel A. Tannenbaum protested against this "tendency to vilify Hamlet."[2] But the protest has failed to deter his detractors. In 1948 Charles A. Dawson stigmatized the Prince as characteristically theatrical and signally inept in his improvisations. Dawson declared: "His scheme of adapting *The Murder of Gonzago* to 'catch the conscience of the king' goes awry. Nothing in the whole drama is more obvious than the failure of the 'mouse trap.'"[3] In 1957 Rebecca West ignored Hamlet's so-called theatricalism but maligned his actions, branding him "an exceptionally callous murderer." Then she added:

> He is an egotist and annuls his natural affections so that he achieves no valid relationship: he is a disobedient son to his father, he defiles his mother, he is a querulous and fugitive lover, he is not a husband and not a father, and he treats Horatio as a listening ear rather than as a friend.[4]

Another school, which credits neither Shakespeare's sense of dramatic purpose nor his genius for character development, has regarded the issues in the play as insoluble. In 1907 W. J. Rolfe stated that "The Hamlet problem has been well called 'the Sphinx of modern literature.'"[5] In 1956 Leo Kirschbaum,[6] endorsing the opinion of Robert Bridges in 1927, concluded that the drama had for its goal the mystification of the audience. In 1961 Weston Babcock in *Hamlet: A Tragedy of Errors* attributed this mystification to flaws or inconsistencies in Shakespeare.

The majority of critics, past and present, have considered the play understandable in other terms. They interpret its protagonist as anything except a doer, claiming that "Hamlet was intended as a warning against hesitation."[7] One group of these critics, utilizing the concepts of psychoanalysis, imputes this assumed hesitancy to the Prince's presumed Oedipus complex. A test of this double-pronged theory forms the basis of Chapters One and Two of this study. Here one may simply note that in 1917 W. W. Greg recorded probably the most extreme psychological diagnosis: "The narrative of the Ghost . . . [is] but a figment of Hamlet's brain."[8]

Meanwhile, the detractors have remained relentless in their disparagement, decrying the hero and applauding the villain. In 1962, for example, Robert Speaight concocted a proposition to undermine the Prince as a worthy witness against his uncle. According to him, Hamlet "suggests" flaws in the King's character which Shakespeare never permits the audience to "see." Then he charged, ". . . there is nothing to show that he seems a monster to anybody else." These accusations contradict the text; namely, the suspicions of Marcellus, the disclosure of the Ghost, the remorse of Claudius himself, the revolt of the Danish populace against the King, and the condemnation by the dying Laertes. The spectators see all this, and they hear and see Hamlet when he vilifies the murderer in Horatio's presence and later in Gertrude's. Since neither of them questions Hamlet's veracity, the evidence against the King scarcely calls for rebuttal. The modern acceptance of Claudius, reminiscent of the Romantic attitude toward Milton's Satan, reaches its apogee in Speaight's startling fallacy: "Claudius has controlled his purpose to an unscrupulous end; Hamlet has no purpose to control."[9]

The chief objective in the study that follows is to restore to Hamlet his good name. Attention centers on razing the false superstructures of these criticisms of Hamlet's character. In their stead, this study introduces a set of approaches based on literary concepts. Chapter Three aims to compare the plot with folklore motifs[10] and medieval conventions that justify Hamlet's course of action. The aim of Chapter Four is to reveal why he repudiates Ophelia. Other aims are to explain how the sinner Gertrude redeems herself, how the Ghost serves as the "mighty opposite"[11] of the new King, and, in Chapter Five, how the Nordic hero

Hamlet evolves from "a dull and muddy-mettled rascal" into a nimble-witted trickster.[12]

At the end of his life Hamlet himself cries out to Horatio for justification:

> O God, Horatio, what a wounded name,
> Things standing thus unknown, shall live behind me!
> If thou didst ever hold me in thy heart,
> Absent thee from felicity a while
> And in this harsh world draw thy breath in pain
> To tell my story (V, ii, 355-360).[13]

CHAPTER ONE

In My Orchard a Serpent

THE traditional interpretation of Shakespeare's *Hamlet* conceived the action as resulting from the hero's simple hesitance. It remained for writers in the twentieth century to distort this widely accepted view. A succession of modern critics have attributed Hamlet's course to procrastination and defective character. In 1919 the eminent scholar Elmer Edgar Stoll branded him guilty of the "sin of inaction."[1] In 1932 the poet T. S. Eliot saw him as "dominated by an emotion" which "remains to poison life and obstruct action."[2] The popular screen version of 1948 featuring Sir Laurence Olivier as the Prince introduced the drama as the story "of a man who couldn't make up his mind."[3] The fault, that is, would lie with Hamlet himself; his failure promptly to execute the orders of his father's ghost would be construed as the behavior of a hero too weak and too undetermined to crystallize his thoughts into action.

This solution of the plot, while it might satisfy the casual beholder of abbreviated acting versions, is not strictly accurate. It disregards elements in the unfolding movement that restrain Hamlet from acting immediately. A more reasonable interpretation would picture Hamlet as the Elizabethan man of melancholy, in which mould he is cast, and his difficulty as that of overcoming a series of obstacles before he can kill Claudius. In surmounting the obstacles, he emulates the Scandinavian archetype of the trickster. These factors, it may well be argued, eventually emerge as more important than his seeming irresoluteness. For much of his ostensible indecisiveness derives from his inability to reconstruct and assimilate at once all of the pre-play political machinations that occurred during his absence from the Danish court. Substantial evidence in the drama supports the theory that much of Hamlet's delay stems from political considerations and is therefore necessary under the circumstances. This evidence affords a logical construction of the character of the hero and repairs some of the damage done to his name.

The first relevant clues in this direction appear in what occurred before the accession of King Claudius. The prerequisite to his election was of course the removal of the elder Hamlet, and for this reason Shakespeare's two accounts of the death of the old King must be plumbed for their full meaning. For, contrary to conventional methods of construction, the dramatic action of *Hamlet* really opens with a corpse, requiring a flashback to unravel the story. As G. Wilson Knight puts it, ". . . the climax is at the start."[4] The simple fact of the entrance of the Ghost in the opening scene divulges to the audience the important circumstance that the ruler of Denmark had died. The drama in effect commences with the events in Denmark which motivated Claudius to resort to murder in order to gain the throne and with the false report of the manner of the death which he, presumably, spread far and wide.

The substance of this rumor, which becomes the pivot in the political affairs of the Danish Kingdom, is that the death of King Hamlet apparently occurred by accident. The misleading story circulated throughout the kingdom claimed that a serpent had mortally stung him while he slept.

> Now, Hamlet, hear:
> 'T is given out that, sleeping in my orchard,
> A serpent stung me; so the whole ear of Denmark
> Is by a forged process of my death
> Rankly abus'd (I, v, 34-38).[5]

The elder Hamlet slept in the orchard every afternoon (I, v, 60). The garden evidently served as the retreat for the King to escape the cares of state and lay aside the stiff dignity of his warrior guise. Both the orchard and the King's naps there would be familiar to the inner circle at the Danish court and in particular to both Claudius and Gertrude.

On the date of the old King's sudden demise,[6] the country was enjoying peace after recent conflicts with Poland and Norway. Denmark, ruled by a valiant sovereign ("For so this side of our known world esteem'd him —" [I, i, 85]), also then occupied a position of supreme power among its neighbors. Throughout an impressive history, the rulers of Denmark had won the reputation of being men of unusual vigor. The imposing physical stature of the senior Hamlet, his "fair and warlike form" (I, i, 47), symbolized the awful majesty of a puissant state. Everyone touted him as a warrior-king. Assuredly he was cultured and affectionate toward his queen, but with these virtues he also displayed the savage traits of his fighting forbears. The kingdom of Hamlet the sovereign everywhere commanded respect for both its culture and its might.

The high regard in which the Danes held King Hamlet may help to explain why they considered his sudden and unexpected end as no more than an unfortunate accident. In a country at peace, who would wish to kill a ruler who so valiantly shepherded his subjects and protected his lands? Since he enjoyed the esteem of his family, courtiers, and people, certainly no one within the boundaries of Denmark would harbor the idea of murdering him. Additionally, his repute as a fearsome warrior would be a formidable safeguard against a spy or an intruder from another country. Further, no problem existed as to the loyalty of his Danish warriors, who were true to a feudal code which required of a soldier that he exact vengeance upon the enemy who dared to assault his lord. Furthermore, treachery of any sort by a lord's retainers carried, in its turn, the odium of the highest crime a vassal might commit.[7]

The news of his father's death, coupled with that of his mother's wedding, summoned Prince Hamlet home. The nobility of other kingdoms also came to pay their respects or to mourn. Hamlet's friend Horatio, a fellow student at Wittenberg, came to Denmark as a mourner. Laertes came from Paris for the nuptials. At this stage, the Danes and their visitors from near and far accepted fully the idea that Hamlet's father had met death by accident in his sleep. This conviction left them free to focus their attention on the marriage as a happy occasion.

The enemy country of Norway, however, had a special interest in the death of the Danish king. In that neighboring land young Prince Fortinbras sensed that more had happened than the passing of a ruler. To him, the death of the Danish sovereign meant not only the lessening of the might and prestige of Denmark but also the end of an epoch. He no doubt perceived that the loss of King

Hamlet would weaken the nature of Danish dominion. At the beginning of the play Claudius senses that Fortinbras has assessed the state of Denmark "to be disjoint and out of frame" (I, ii, 20). It also would reasonably occur to Fortinbras that he at last might regain for Norway the prestige it had lost when his father died in battle by the sword of Hamlet's father.[8] Had there been any suspicion that someone had murdered the Danish king, Fortinbras would have been the leading and logical suspect. Had he killed the Dane, it would have been a simple instance of a blood feud[9] in which a son avenged his sire.

There must have existed, then, a strong reason why Prince Fortinbras escaped suspicion. There was. The explanation is that the Danes had evidently accepted a cause of death that better fitted the circumstances. They made no error in their supposition: they reasoned that poison had caused their late King's death. Their ground for so believing was the appearance presented by the corpse. The condition of the body, wholly covered with scaly scabs, a "vile and loathsome crust" (I, v, 72), would make poisoning self-evident. A mysterious agent had entered the blood stream and permeated the epidermis. Its origin was not of course equally obvious; however, an entirely natural conjecture would be that some insect or creature of the orchard had bitten the royal Dane. But no sign of a bite or laceration of the skin could be found. A beast would be dismissed as a possible assailant because it leaves toothmarks, and no such telltale signs existed. Insects would be ruled out for a different reason; namely, their venom is not strong enough to cause death. The report which gained ready acceptance was poisoning by the "sting" of a serpent.[10] This explanation for the spoiled condition of the body appears sound enough. First, the venom of a serpent has power enough to be fatal; second, the marks of a serpent's fangs would not be detectable beneath the poisoned crusts about the corpse. And the Danes were nearly right. Poison had killed their monarch. They correctly named the application; they incorrectly identified its applier.

As for the reaction to his death, the elder Hamlet received eulogies because he was a strong king, not simply because the mourners waxed sentimental over a deceased personage. Often the dead take on a virtue and a glory which they never possessed in life; the noble deeds of this king were fully authenticated. There remains the possibility that this war hero was more respected than loved. Since he often left court for battle, his wife may have pined for affection during his long absences. Moreover, a paragon is, of all people, the one person most difficult to abide; and a commanding sovereign easily can fall victim to his own arrogance and imperiousness. If Hamlet's father owned these ugly attributes, such distasteful behavior may have estranged Queen Gertrude. But positively no proof exists that the royal victim had alienated the loyalty of any one of his subjects; nobody, in fact, had just cause for doing away with him.

Not the slightest clue had been left in the orchard to incriminate a human being. Claudius had skilfully plotted a perfect murder. No human agent, not even the injured Prince robbed of elevation to the throne, suspected Claudius of the crime. It requires in the play the supernatural aid of the Ghost to disclose what really had occurred, to name the crime and identify its perpetrator.

> . . . know, thou noble youth,
> The serpent that did sting thy father's life
> Now wears his crown (I, v, 38-40).

Meanwhile, the Danes unquestioningly attributed the King's death to the accidental bite of an actual snake. They reached the only conclusion that agreed with the facts available at the time of their observation. After all, they had heard nothing of a ghost and had seen nothing irregular in the King's death.

By the wintertime date that Hamlet reached home, the explanation that his father had met accidental death was already accepted and well entrenched. The talk of courtiers at Elsinore no doubt would include such usual generalizations as how death comes upon a person when he is about his routine duties, when in the midst of life, or, as here, when asleep. Perhaps someone may have noted the irony of a warrior-king's dying, not in the thick of battle, but in his sleep unarmored. No further inquiry was in order.

Matters had apparently been settled once and for all by the official version of poison and serpent. This version would gain wide circulation because of the eminence of the deceased and become firmly lodged in the minds of its hearers. A weighty fact is that no suspicion of Claudius on the part of the populace ever arises until the final scene of the play. One of the laws of communication asserts the virtual impossibility of supplanting a credible first story with a second and later explanation.

If the Danish citizens had no suspicions, how did the royal guards react to the news? These palace warders had a special bond of loyalty to their leader in being personally responsible for his safety. They would have been more stricken by his death than the mass of Danish subjects, who enjoyed no similar personal ties with the King. In the opening scene of the drama, Bernardo comes on a bitterly cold night to relieve the guard Francisco. It may be sympathy for his lord that prompts Francisco to remark that "I am sick at heart" (I, i, 8). The statement by itself seems to have no other meaning.[11] The drama divulges no personal tragedy in his life to explain why he is sorrowing.

It may be crucial to the meaning that Francisco's fellow warders do not question or challenge his statement; instead, they accept it without comment or reply. The Ghost has already twice appeared to them, and possibly Francisco's heart sickens because he fears that his lord has met with foul play and that he and his fellows might have been somehow blameworthy in not having shielded their departed King. On the other hand, if this thought occurs to them or if anybody asks them about intruders, they can testify that they have seen no invader crossing the boundary under their surveillance. The guard Francisco vanishes from the stage after the first scene, so that what he knew, suspected, or felt can only be surmised. His failure later to voice his opinions denies the audience the opportunity to examine this first-hand observer who lived close to King Hamlet. His complete disappearance considerably heightens the mystery of *Hamlet*. In view of these facts, at this point Francisco's declaration is difficult to construe as anything except an allusion to the fact that his heart is filled with grief. But perhaps a look at subsequent happenings may help to clarify what he means.

A little later, when Hamlet sees the Ghost, he departs with him for further parley, leaving behind him his companions, Horatio and the guard Marcellus. The faithful Marcellus, suggesting "Let's follow" (I, iv, 88), shows himself apprehensive for Hamlet's safety. More to the point, he believes that the Ghost's appearance betokens some dire event, for he says, "Something is rotten in the state of Denmark" (I, iv, 90). The bold disparagement in Marcellus' words,[12] a specific censure by a feudal officer, of moral decadence in Elsinore has much more portent than the painfully subjective declaration of the soldier Francisco. The officer Marcellus, it becomes clear, suspects that some dreadful crisis confronts the Danish realm. This later unmistakable suspicion on the part of Marcellus may help to explain the earlier perturbation of Francisco. The two men would of course have discussed the King's death. To their knowledge, no trespasser ever ventured into the precincts which they patrol. Thus, if an assassin has committed regicide, he has to be a Dane in "the state of Denmark." Viewed in this light, Francisco's sickness at heart takes on an added meaning. Perhaps he is sick with suspicion, not grief. So interpreted, these scenes offer evidence that both Francisco and Marcellus have begun to doubt that their King died by accident. If they do have doubts, Hamlet's subsequent report of what the Ghost tells him would prove their suppositions to be correct.

Like Francisco, Marcellus disappears from the stage after Act One. Though Claudius may suspect them, there is no certain testimony that he dismisses them from his retinue. Nonetheless, they patently are suspicious. In this connection, Shakespeare may have a primary artistic motive for their disappearance. They may be discarded in order to focus upon Hamlet as the sole investigator for unraveling the mystery. Horatio, to be sure, recognizes the Ghost as the late King and suspects a political machination, since he observes in his first encounter with the apparition that "in the gross and scope of mine opinion,/This bodes some strange eruption to our state" (I, i, 68-69). These suspicions enable Hamlet later to enlist Horatio's aid more than once in the investigation, but he hides from both Francisco and Marcellus his own disquieting suspicions aroused by the Ghost. The Prince himself, as dramatically proper, always discharges the major role. That part in the early acts demands not an avenger but a detective.

What other data Hamlet gleans from Horatio and the royal guards, the play fails to elaborate; but the Ghost gives his son exact details. Murder has been done; the specter of the old King says that he died, not by the sting of a serpent, but by the hand of his brother Claudius.

Claudius had taken his brother Hamlet's life by pouring a poison into the ear of the sleeping King.

> Sleeping within mine orchard,
> My custom always of the afternoon,
> Upon my secure hour thy uncle stole,
> With juice of cursed hebona in a vial,
> And in the porches of mine ears did pour
> The lep'rous distilment; whose effect
> Holds such an enmity with blood of man
> That swift as quicksilver it courses through
> The natural gates and alleys of the body,
> And with a sudden vigour it doth posset
> And curd, like eager droppings into milk,
> The thin and wholesome blood: so did it mine,
> And a most instant tetter bark'd about,
> Most lazar-like, with vile and loathsome crust,
> All my smooth body (I, v, 59-73).

The main question raised by this description is how Claudius could introduce the "hebona" into the sleeping man's blood stream without waking him. As there were no signs of a struggle, the victim presumably did not awaken but learned the identity of his murderer by the supernatural power of divination. A secondary question is, What poison[13] could have produced such a violent skin reaction? In answer, perhaps Shakespeare's description of the poison and its effects is purely imaginative. Had Prince Hamlet studied the rudiments of either anatomy or medicine, it seems that he might have asked the Ghost these questions. Instead, he voices no disbelief whatever, and if he has doubts, he keeps them to himself. Whether the description be viewed either imaginatively or realistically, the physical appearance of the dead King was rendered repulsive to the sight. Claudius perpetrated a murder horrendous in its externals, one calculated to appall the beholder of the corpse. When Gertrude saw the body of her spouse covered with a "vile and loathsome crust," how much more attractive Claudius would appear to her.

Another shocking aspect of the crime is that it represents an unnatural murder. The slaying of brother by brother, of Hamlet by Claudius, came into the world as "the primal eldest curse"

(III, iii, 37). The Bible states: "And it came to pass, when they were in the field, that Cain rose up against Abel and slew him" (Genesis, 4:2).

Had the Ghost named young Fortinbras as the assassin, Prince Hamlet would have called the act the fortunes of war and exacted his revenge as soon as practicable. But as the drama opens, Denmark is enjoying peace, although the military officials know that the Norwegian prince has "Shark'd up a list of lawless resolutes" (I, i, 98) and may be bent on recovering territories his father lost to the Danes. The public disclosure in Act V that the killing was a depraved murder, a fratricide, shows that the state has rotted at its head. The Danish prince learns this secret in Act I. To a reflective hero like him, the Ghost's revelation that his uncle Claudius is the assassin may not come as altogether a surprise. Overcome as he is by grief, he yet notes with alarm how hastily his mother wedded Claudius, observing that "the funeral bak'd-meats/Did coldly furnish forth the marriage tables" (I, ii, 180-181). Horatio agrees that the marriage had "followed hard upon" the funeral (I, ii, 179), but nobody else speaks of the marriage as hasty. Its hurried performance so soon after his father's death distresses the son greatly and manifestly first arouses his suspicions of Claudius. What now would agitate the Prince even more would be the discovery that the revelations of the Ghost and the hasty marriage confirm his worst fears.

The appearance of the Ghost seems to have terrified the guards. They think the apparition may be an evil spirit, noting that "when the cock crew./. . . it started like a guilty thing/Upon a fearful summons" (I, i, 147-149). They also wonder, nervously, about what they may be called upon to do as fighting men. Marcellus wants to know why

> So nightly toils the subject of the land,
> And why such daily cast of brazen cannon,
> And foreign mart for implements of war;
> Why such impress of shipwrights, whose sore task
> Does not divide the Sunday from the week (I, i, 72-76).

When the guards appeal to Horatio for explication, he tells Marcellus that Denmark is preparing for an attack by the Norse prince:

> Now, sir, young Fortinbras,
> Of unimproved mettle hot and full,
> Hath in the skirts of Norway here and there
> Shark'd up a list of lawless resolutes,
> For food and diet, to some enterprise
> That hath a stomach in 't (I, i, 95-100).

After this explanation, the soldiers sensibly interpret the specter as an omen of danger for Denmark, for Horatio asks the Ghost:

> If thou art privy to thy country's fate,
> Which, happily, foreknowing may avoid,
> O speak! (I, i, 133-135).

Hamlet, in turn, does not entertain similar superstitions about the Ghost [14] and betrays no fear equal to theirs in either meeting his father's shade or walking off with him. Neither does Hamlet ask why the King's spirit has appeared. Why, then, does the Prince not move at once? For one thing, he has a hard course thrust upon him when the Ghost obliges him to discard the accepted evidence and prevailing view of his sire's death. Act II introduces another reason for the hero's inaction. There he tends to discount the specter's unsupported testimony because ghosts were traditionally held to be in league with the Devil.

Then Hamlet has sound reasons within himself for delaying his decisions. A major problem lies in proving the guilt of his uncle Claudius: as a Christian, Hamlet, the nephew, needs data to supplement the testimony of his father's spirit; as a scholar, he has to proceed logically and develop a clear case of murder against the usurper; and as a practical man, he cannot kill Claudius without a proof of guilt, since he than might himself be considered a murderer. For another inner difficulty, the specter's full account might be understood to implicate Gertrude as an accomplice, for the Ghost says that the "adulterate beast" Claudius has fired her with lust:

> So lust, though to a radiant angel link'd,
> Will sate itself in a celestial bed
> And prey on garbage (I, v, 55-57).

The situation, so delineated, sows a serious doubt in Hamlet's mind about his mother. The Ghost, however, restricts his son to working vengeance against Claudius alone:

> But, howsomever thou pursuest this act,
> Taint not thy mind, nor let thy soul contrive
> Against thy mother aught: leave her to heaven
> And to those thorns that in her bosom lodge,
> To prick and sting her (I, v, 84-88).

Does the Ghost mean by this that Gertrude is innocent of murder, that he is ignorant of the degree of her complicity, that he regards his finite son as a misogynist, or that he knows her guilty but wishes his son to spare her?[15]

In the French version by Belleforest,[16] Hamlet's father marries Gertrude, who as the daughter of a king would succeed him, thus spoiling the succession for his brother. If Shakespeare had this pattern in mind, then Hamlet ought to have been elected sovereign upon the demise of his father. If the dynasty maintained itself through the queen, then Gertrude would have been ruler of the land for the interval of "a little month" (I, ii, 147) before she took unto herself a consort,[17] who in turn would become king. If Claudius claimed the throne by right of descent after his brother, then he could have been elected monarch by the court councilors.[18]

In the play itself Claudius regards Gertrude as sharing the throne equally with him: on his accession, he addresses her as "our sometimes sister, now our queen,/Th' imperial jointress to this warlike state" (I, ii, 8-9). Probably he married her for political advantage as well as for love. Possibly the electors of the Danish court believed that Claudius was a strong man and that they should install him in the kingship to quell the growing threat from Norway. Perhaps they disregarded Hamlet, not because he was away at Wittenberg but because they deemed him too young and unproved in war to become their monarch. In flat opposition to this last premise stands the fact that young, untried Fortinbras, replacing his ailing uncle, rules over Norway successfully enough to raise a new band against the Danes (I, i, 69-104). The impression one receives is that the capabilities of Hamlet, a fit foil to youthful Norway, were wrongly assessed or purposely overlooked.

It is true, however, that the Ghost, eager for quick revenge, makes no mention of Hamlet's being cheated of the throne and addresses him as a "youth" (I, v, 38). The late King certainly uses every rhetorical device at his command to whet Hamlet's appetite for shedding blood. The phantom, in his several appearances to the Prince, paints Claudius in blackest hue. The father's failure to sympathize with his son on the score of the Prince's deprivation appears somewhat remarkable, as indeed does Hamlet's own failure to broach the matter, unless of course they both regard the injustice as too rank to require special mention. Evidently the sire has more concern for redressing the wrongs done to himself than for gaining the throne for his son. Besides, if the son now sought to gain the crown, he might be slain in this bold process and the father robbed of his vengeance. The Ghost, at best, impresses one throughout as egocentric, rather jealous, and indifferent to the fate of either his lineal heir or the kingdom of Denmark.

Everything in Elsinore happened fast, too quickly for Hamlet, then away at Wittenberg, to prevent Gertrude's remarriage or to influence Claudius's accession. At the outset of the action, it is the hasty marriage which disturbs the Prince. He grew up under his mother's influence rather than that of his father, who often busied himself with battles in distant lands (I, i, 61-63). Hamlet describes his mother as of a warm, affectionate — even sensual — nature (I, ii, 143-145). Obviously neglected to some degree by her peregrinating first husband, Gertrude may have been starved for affection or given to lust. The Ghost never specifically accuses her of adultery, but he does something tantamount to this when he labels her partner "that adulterate beast" (I, v, 41). The Ghost's wrath abates with respect to her; in place of accusing her as one of his slayers, he orders Hamlet not to harm her.

The chief, if not indeed the only, complaint against Hamlet's hesitancy comes from the ghostly Dane. Impetuous in life, as shown when "in angry parle,/He smote the sledded Polacks on the ice" (I, i, 62-63), the apparition of the King demands prompt retribution. The warlike sire wants blood for blood. For a spirit, he shows a human jealousy of his widow. He suffers agony in thinking of her in "shameful lust" (I, v, 45) with his brother, demanding that an immediate end be put to their cohabitation. Under the circumstances, the grieving Prince seems to act normally and with fine intelligence in assembling proof of the crime. His grief abates when he recognizes the import of the Ghost's declarations. That is, the Prince himself now can develop the case against the usurping couple. He seizes upon this unexpected supernatural corroboration of his direst suspicions as a decisive incentive for moving at once against Claudius.

Like Saxo's Amleth, from whom he descended, by his "skilful defence of himself, and strenuous revenge for his parent, he has left it doubtful whether we are to think more of his wit or his bravery."[19] In the play, Hamlet's merciless repartee soon begins to take effect on Claudius, whom he excels in combats of deceit, until the new King loses his suavity and drops his ingratiating tone. The King reveals the extent of his defeat when he kneels contritely in prayer. The Prince's brilliant sallies of wit vie for the admiration of the audience with his bravery in the duel with Laertes. As for his verbal exchanges with his father's spirit, Hamlet behaves equally sensibly: he never once argues with the Ghost, placates him with promises, or says him nay. Instead, he goes about solving the problem thrust upon him in a manner wholly rational, deliberate, and expedient.

A vindication of his method can be found in the figure of Horatio, Hamlet's closest friend. Horatio is one with whom the Prince can and does talk freely. They discuss the first appearances of the Ghost; afterward, Hamlet further informs his friend of the murder and how it was done. Later on, the Prince requests and receives Horatio's aid as observer of the reactions of Claudius to the play-within-the-play. Later still, they discuss Hamlet's sea voyage and its aftermath, as well as the new plot by Claudius for pitting Hamlet against Laertes in a duel. But at no time during frequent heart-to-heart talks does Horatio ever so much as intimate hesitance on Hamlet's part. Never once does this sole confidant urge the avenger to act with more dispatch. Since they converse at length on sundry matters, this silence of Horatio seems to mean that he approves of his friend's conduct. The Ghost alone waxes importunate, but this offended Ghost is a prejudiced party. His manifest jealousy of the Queen renders his several reentries open to question as reliable evidence of the Prince's alleged procrastination.

Strong reasons dictate the mode of Hamlet's managing his vengeance. He desires to establish the crime of murder against his uncle. He wishes to prove the guilt or innocence of his mother, and he wants to know what evil coterie surrounds Claudius. All of the facts have to be marshaled before he can proceed. To kill Claudius and miss other possible conspirators would risk the Prince's life prematurely and jeopardize his hope of meeting his filial obligation.

Such deliberation requires reflection and time in abundance. Hamlet's so-called delay has therefore been widely misconstrued. The matters which he feels obliged to settle can not easily be resolved, but he works on them with a will throughout the play. Every time he comes on stage he is busy: interrogating others, acting out prearranged roles, avoiding devices to entrap him, plying a double-edged wit, adding lines to the play-within-the-play, planning with Horatio, pretending one thing and saying another. Even in his self-critical soliloquies, where he appears to be weak and vacillating, the problem of his vengeance remains uppermost in his mind. The long passages portraying his irresolution and "pale cast" of thinking resemble the devices of Scandinavian trickery.[20] When alone, he rails against his indecisiveness; when with others, he plots with craftiness. This contrast between word and deed enforces the sense of irony which pervades Shakespeare's drama.

In Act I the Prince actually accomplishes a great deal. He determines to his seeming satisfaction that the death of his father did not occur by accident. He also secures evidence as to the identity of the killer. The only issue he still has to face is the perplexing problem of his mother, which the Ghost introduces. Shall he "leave her to heaven" or search out the truth? Hamlet's conscience demands the truth, and the truth cannot be quickly rooted out. Further, his uncle's outrageous crime calls for an equivalent revenge,[21] which the prompt thrust of a rapier can hardly accomplish.

CHAPTER TWO

O Most Pernicious Woman

 MODERN hypothesis has arisen in support of the traditional view of Hamlet's alleged lethargy. It is based on a psychoanalytical approach wherein abnormality could account for the procrastination imputed to the Prince; namely, an immature overdependence on his mother. Hamlet's ruminations about Gertrude hardly seem unusual under the circumstances of his recent bereavement, but his emotions have been construed as aberrant by the Freudian school. These interpreters have gone to Greek literature for an ancient parallel in Oedipus Rex, who, without knowing his mother's identity, mated with her. Sigmund Freud's *Interpretation of Dreams* takes the extreme position that "Hamlet is able to do anything but take vengeance upon the man who did away with his father and has taken his father's place with his mother — the man who shows him in realization the repressed desires of his own childhood."[1]

Freud, says the literary critic Jack N. Renfrow, expresses as consciousness what in Hamlet remained unconscious.[2] In Ernest Jones's recent *Hamlet and Oedipus* Shakespeare's hero, crippled with a "specific aboulia," becomes disgusted with Gertrude's second marriage. The son discovers that the match has forced into the foreground his own infantile sexual longings which he has hitherto repressed.[3]

Noel Coward's drama *The Vortex* introduces a weakling son as a kind of literary descendant of Hamlet. Coward's Nicky Lancaster exhibits a morbid emotional reliance on his philandering mother and descends to drug addiction. The characterization of Nicky derives from the widespread interpretation of the Prince as immaturely attached to his mother. The Oedipus theory enthralls yet another imaginative writer: in the poem "The Shepherd" Hyam Plutzik's Ambleth "seized his mother and ravished her/(Unknowing, of course)."[4]

In *Dark Legend,* a sociological study by the psychiatrist Dr. Frederic Wertham, the Danish Prince embodies instead the classical legend of Orestes. Dr. Wertham defines the Orestes complex as the "dynamic transformation of an over-attachment to the mother-image into hostility against her."[5] He further detects homosexual potentialities in Hamlet. Yet other exponents of this concept, making much of Hamlet's "Man delights not me" attribute outright homosexuality to the Prince,[6] ignoring the self-explanatory words that come next, "nor woman neither, though by your smiling you seem to say so" (II, ii, 322-324). They hold in particular that Ophelia's grave symbolizes a vagina and that when Hamlet jumps into the grave, he discloses his homosexual inclination toward her brother Laertes.[7]

In opposition to these psychoanalytical postulates, there is the simple alternative of scrutinizing Hamlet's behavior literally for a less strained explication of his relations with his mother. One of the Ghost's two commands touches on this very point. The first injunction, as already seen, requires the Prince to "Revenge his foul and most unnatural murder" (I, v, 25). The second, "Let not the royal bed of Denmark be/A couch for luxury and damned incest" (I, v, 82-83), may be read as invoking a normal son's reaction to his mother's marriage to his father's only brother. So interpreted, this second demand is harder than the first, since it orders Hamlet not to execute his mother but rather to redeem her by persuasion or appeal to her reason. The son, not knowing the extent of her involvement in the assassination, can not straightway disclose to her the Ghost's confidences. To do so would place his life in immediate jeopardy, as she of course might repeat these suspicions to the murderous Claudius. Not out of fear of death itself (I, iv, 65) but from desire to honor his pledge to his father, the son must stay alive to exact final vengeance.

This dilemma makes the Prince's problem all the harder. He needs adducible evidence against his uncle before acting, since he evidently does not wish to construct his case solely on the Ghost's revelations. The Ghost from his infinite world could be held a biased witness on the ground that he hated his finite brother Claudius for hastily marrying his widow; or a diabolical and untrustworthy witness on the basis of his supernormal origin. At the end of Act II, Hamlet still debates the credibility of the Ghost's accusations.

> The spirit that I have seen
> May be a devil; and the devil hath power
> T' assume a pleasing shape; yea, and perhaps
> Out of my weakness and my melancholy,
> As he is very potent with such spirits,
> Abuses me to damn me (II, ii, 627-632).

The son's other difficulty lies in his natural disinclination to injure Gertrude, particularly since he seems uncertain whether his mother had been unfaithful to his father.

Since the Ghost's words may imply two orders, Hamlet faces a choice. Shall he immediately execute the usurper with his bloodletting sword, or shall he take time to redeem his mother with his chastening tongue? In the play Hamlet does save his mother first. In doing so, he is today discredited by numberless critics as a mollycoddled psychopath rather than appreciated as an exemplar of filial concern. But demands of Shakespeare's artistry enter here. Had Hamlet waited to save her soul until after dispatching Claudius, no dramatic effect could have resulted. This would have represented no redemption and would have robbed Gertrude of a choice.

The devotion of this son to his mother had been solidly nourished in their earliest association. He had grown to manhood largely under her guidance and influence, since wars with neighboring Norway and Poland (I, i, 61-63) kept his father away from home. He voices much respect, admiration, and some true affection for his father; but, after King Hamlet's death, the thoughts which most agitate the son's heart center always on his mother. The Prince, nonetheless, betrays no effeminacy in either his appearance or his personal habits. It is the long work of adding datum to data, not cowardice and not effeminate aversion to bloodshed, which postpone the hour of his vengeance. But no doubt, as a child, he learned something about feminine wiles from being associated with his mother and women of the court. Gertrude's penchant for prevarication leads her to report falsely to Laertes his sister's suicide as an accidental death. He also in childhood would have acquired a knack for masquerade from such a master as the court jester Yorick.

From all these sources, he seems to have gained an extraordinary knowledge of women (III, i, 148-157). The most useful thing he learned was the trick of dissembling, which the female proverbially has fashioned into a fine art. In *Hamlet* the hero's feigned madness is like a harlot's painted face. It serves as a disguise. His effective camouflage owes much to an acquaintance with the subtleties of women's ways. To a perceptible degree, he knows how women think.

Many of his soliloquies reflect sham emotionalism. He always busies himself on the stage when in the presence of others, but, when alone, he laments the irresoluteness with which he taxes himself. These scenes of criticisms of self, following hard on scenes of activity, have a definitely ironic ring.[8] This element of satire affords relief in a preponderantly brooding tragedy: it combats the saccharinity which might otherwise pervade the story of a son's veneration for his father's memory and concern for his mother's misdoings. This should put the quietus on efforts to read into Hamlet's conduct a perverted attitude toward his mother's person.

His attitude, a normal one, is that of an indignant son and heir. He waxes savage, dwelling vulgarly in sensual symbols on the mating of mother and uncle.

> Nay, but to live
> In the rank sweat of an enseamed bed,
> Stew'd in corruption, honeying and making love
> Over the nasty sty— (III, iv, 91-94).

Hamlet does not remain preoccupied with Gertrude because of an abnormal interest in her, but because he chooses to deal with her salvation before disposing of Claudius. Here he manifests a son's accepted regard for a parent's well-being. His father is dead beyond requickening, but his mother yet lives and so could be salvaged. His task, a special one, is to show her the evil of her present estate and to persuade her to relinquish it. The psychoanalytical school, on the contrary, maintains that he can not and does not move against the Queen because his Oedipus complex reduces him to the status of a child emotionally dependent on his mother.

In Greek drama, the equally famous *Electra* also invites comparison. There the Furies hound Orestes to avenge the death of his father by slaying his mother, and he does so as their instrument. Does the Danish prince similarly contemplate killing his mother? The cases are distinctly not parallel. The circumstances of Hamlet's commission, it should be noted, require of him a single, not a double, execution. In the flow of his worried cogitations as the moral agent of a vengeful God, he may have contemplated the frightful possibility of being required to put his mother to death. His father's spirit appears to suspect this direction in his son's thoughts when he cautions him to leave his mother "to heaven" (I, v, 86). In this presumed quandary resides an analogy, not with Oedipus Rex but with Orestes, who slays his mother.

At face value, the analogies of both Oedipus and Orestes appear provocative, but does Hamlet have their same motives? Does he lust for his mother like Oedipus? Is he determined to kill his mother like Orestes? The inappropriateness of the Greek plays as models comes unmistakably to light when one reviews the relation of Hamlet to the Queen.

The Prince's problem is to alienate his mother from his uncle, but he has no proof of what had occurred between them after he went to Wittenberg. No specific reference in the play to Gertrude herself proves that she engaged in an affair with Claudius before King Hamlet's murder, but other statements make her adultery an inescapable inference. The Ghost stigmatizes Claudius as an adulterer, thereby imputing infidelity to the partner in sin. Irrespective of the degree and duration of the illicit intimacy, Hyam Plutzik unquestionably overdraws the situation. In "The Shepherd," previously quoted, the adulterer sires the Prince during the old King's absence at war. It nonetheless seems unlikely that Claudius would have resorted to fratricide if he had not already won the affections of the Queen. Through her he became the new ruler of Denmark. It thus may have been their lust for each other which first gave the brother his ambition for the crown and his impulse to murder. Earlier she had evidently loved King Hamlet

(I, ii, 143-145). How, then, could she later have lost feeling for him? He had grown old and probably had dissipated much of his potency in devotion to the battlefield. Moreover, his repeated absences from home probably led him to forget, or to neglect, the niceties which women crave. As Ghost, he always has a most superior air about him, declaring himself by comparison with Claudius the owner of rich "natural gifts" (I, v, 51). As living man, he dealt directly with his critics and confronted his enemies openly; he was a man's man, not a woman's. So much superciliousness in a man might awe a slave but would rather repel the Queen as a woman. The day that Gertrude saw him as a disfigured corpse in the orchard, she may even have felt revulsion.

Claudius, a younger man than King Hamlet, had youth enough to win Gertrude for his wife before the play opens. His flattering speeches to her in *Hamlet* attest that he has not forgotten the manner and blandishments which melt the feminine heart. He possesses a sparkle, what the Ghost labels a "witchcraft of his wit" (I, v, 43). The Ghost, serious and somber, complains that his brother, convivial and suave, had wooed the Queen assiduously; had presented her with gifts "that have the power/So to seduce" (I, v, 44-45). Confined to a lonely life at court when Hamlet's father followed the wars, the warmhearted Gertrude may have often found pleasure in the company of her spouse's younger brother. Throughout the play Claudius displays nothing but affection for Gertrude; before the curtain, perhaps his love for her weighed as heavily in the balance as his lust for the crown. Although Claudius personifies a Machiavellian master of deceit, his tenderness toward Gertrude seems genuine enough.

The Bible establishes a respected precedent for a man's espousing his brother's relict.[9] But it is the haste of this marriage that arouses the disgust and suspicion of Hamlet. Psychoanalysts might maintain that his preoccupation in his soliloquies with this affront to his father's memory represents a switch in his allegiance, a turning in his emotional dependence from the mother to the father image. But once more, Hamlet's behavior explains itself in terms of his bereavement. A son naturally inclines to dwell on the virtues of his deceased parent in deserved homage to the dead. Whatever hostility he feels for his mother and his irritation at the "wicked speed" which led her to "incestuous sheets" (I, ii, 156-

157) appear both human and normal. None of Hamlet's behavior reflects the so-called negative Oedipus complex, whereby a traumatic experience switches affection from one parent to the other. He might revert to his father's remembrance for strength, but would hardly turn to the apparition for a being on whom to shower his affection. After all, he has no need of an outlet for his love. It would be absurd to forget, amid the theory-spinning, that he already has a sweetheart, "pretty Ophelia" (IV, v, 56).

A more realistic approach would present the Ghost's revelations as intentionally calculated to channel Hamlet's sympathies toward his abused father. The Ghost wholly absolves himself, utterly damning his brother who

> — won to his shameful lust
> The will of my most seeming-virtuous queen;
> O Hamlet, what a falling-off was there!
> From me, whose love was of that dignity
> That it went hand in hand even with the vow
> I made to her in marriage, and to decline
> Upon a wretch whose natural gifts were poor
> To those of mine! (I, v, 45-52).

By this means, the specter accomplishes two ends; first, he inspires his son to pity his dead father; and, second, to exact condign revenge.

In analyzing the Ghost's references to Gertrude, nothing in Shakespeare's text justifies the belief that the sire withholds information from his son. His rhetoric spends itself in provoking the Prince to action. It would therefore be erroneous to assume that Gertrude was an accomplice in the murder, that the Ghost knew it, and that he kept this knowledge secret[10] to prevent his son from shedding his mother's blood. The sum that one gleans from all the innuendoes is that Claudius alone poured a lethal poison in the ear of the sleeping King.

Hamlet nonetheless entertains doubts about his mother's guilt. But he has to get proof from another source, because the Ghost refuses to testify further against her and warns him against thoughts of matricide. Seeking to restrain the Prince, the supernormal visitant gives him an explicit warning: "Taint not thy mind, nor let thy soul contrive/Against thy mother aught" (I, v, 85-86).

Unless he disobeys this injunction, how can he "catch the conscience" of the Queen? He also has an additional assignment to perform. He has to induce his mother to abandon the couch of Claudius; the Ghost expressly exhorts his son not to permit "the royal bed of Denmark" to serve lechery (I, v, 82). To do so, Hamlet has to find a device whereby he can awaken the remorse of the Queen.

The Prince seizes upon the visit of the Players to Elsinore as an opportunity to verify or invalidate the charges of the Ghost. Characteristically, he does not proceed to the business broadside but instead dissembles. He adds lines of his own invention to their speeches, soliloquizing that he will employ their performance to ensnare the King, not the Queen.

> — the play's the thing
> Wherein I'll catch the conscience of the King
>   (II, ii, 633-634).

Note that Hamlet first specifically enjoins Horatio to scan every reaction of Claudius.

> I prithee, when thou seest that act a-foot,
> Even with the very comment of thy soul
> Observe my uncle: if his occulted guilt
> Do not itself unkennel in one speech,
> It is a damned ghost that we have seen,
> And my imaginations are as foul
> As Vulcan's stithy (III, ii, 83-89).

Note also that Hamlet then assures his friend that "I mine eyes will rivet to his face" (III, ii, 90). Does the Prince mean what he says here or does he proceed to dissemble again? The answer, as will be seen, is that he dissembles. This circumstance entitles one to inquire if the intercalary play is designed to apprehend Claudius or to stir remorse in Gertrude and exonerate her.

At this stage of the play's action Hamlet has small doubt about the guilt of his uncle. Doubts about the extent of his mother's complicity now trouble him. In his eyes, her relationship with the King demonstrate emotionality, not rationality. Her heart had prevailed over her head. For this reason, Gertrude forms a fitting counterpart to "the mobled queen," the player with her head swathed. As early as Act II, where the traveling actors recite sample lines, the First Player says, " 'But who, Ah, woe! had seen the mobled queen' " (II, ii, 525). Hamlet promptly senses the aptness of the phrase, repeating it after the player as a question, " 'The mobled queen'?"

In keeping with this concept, note that later, in Act III, the Player Queen accordingly figures more prominently in the opening dumb show than the poisoner. This player, who corresponds to Claudius, simply comes in, takes off the Player King's crown, "kisses it, pours poison in the sleeper's ears, and leaves him." By contrast, the Queen corresponding to Gertrude has the dominant role, and her warm affection for her King is depicted in the major scene of the speechless show.

> Enter a King and Queen, the Queen embracing him and he her. She kneels and makes show of protestation unto him; he takes her up and declines his head upon her neck. He lays him down upon a bank of flowers. She, seeing him asleep, leaves him (III, ii, 145 ff).

After this pantomime comes a prologue of three lines. Here Hamlet has in mind the inconstancy of woman, for he asks Ophelia, "Is this a prologue, or the posy of a ring?" Her reply, " 'T is brief, my lord," the Prince counters with "As woman's love" (III, ii, 162-164). His use of the singular form may again refer to Gertrude, not all womankind, and to her love for King Hamlet as "brief" as a "prologue."

When the ensuing playlet opens, the Player Queen again takes the spotlight, and it is she who first mentions murder. She thrice refers to the situation of a wife made a widow:

> In second husband let me be accurst,
> None wed the second but who killed the first (III, ii, 189-195).

> A second time I kill my husband dead,
> When second husband kisses me in bed (III, ii, 194-195).

> Both here and hence pursue me lasting strife,
> If, once a widow, ever I be wife! (III, ii, 232-233).

Had Gertrude been guilty, these instances would have struck home. Throughout, Hamlet does not "rivet" his "eyes" on Claudius, as he has promised. Instead, he has been glancing at Gertrude. Accordingly, at the end of the passages portraying the guilt of the Player Queen, he exclaims: "If she should break it now!" (III, ii, 234). The burden of all these speeches suggests that Hamlet is testing Gertrude more than Claudius. Significantly also, it is to his mother, not his uncle, that he turns with the query, "Madam, how like you this play?" (III, ii, 239).

The end result of the enactment of "The Murder of Gonzago," or "The Mouse-trap," gives Hamlet his first evidence that Gertrude is no murderess. Hamlet's word for her is "mouse," an endearing term for a woman, as he warns her not to permit Claudius to chamber with her or "call you his mouse" (III, iv, 183). In other words, the Prince does not unsuccessfully bait the "trap" with his mother to capture his uncle; instead, he successfully sets it to "catch" Gertrude, who quickly grasps that something is amiss when she views, "The Mouse-trap." This begins to assert itself when she remarks that she thinks the Player Queen "doth protest too much" (III, ii, 240).

Shortly afterward, she summons Hamlet to her closet. He foregoes an opportunity to slay Claudius when chancing upon him in prayer and proceeds to his mother's chambers. There she greets him with words emblematic of innocence when she says, "Hamlet, thou hast thy father much offended" (III, iv, 9). At this point Gertrude mistakes his intentions, thinking he means her bodily harm, and begins to call for help. When Polonius stirs behind the arras, Hamlet stabs him to death. The Queen protests against the "rash and bloody deed," which prompts him to retort, "A bloody deed — almost as bad, good mother,/As kill a king, and marry with his brother" (III, iv, 28-29). Now Gertrude's innocence expresses itself in astonishment: "As kill a king!" (III, iv, 30). When he straightway accuses her of conspiring with Claudius, he can elicit no more. Her savage inquisitor presses her, "O shame! where is thy blush?" (III, iv, 82).

Gertrude's failure to blush impresses Hamlet as a token of her truthfulness. Having said, "I set you up a glass/Where you may see the inmost part of you" (III, iv, 19-20), he is now satisfied that she has passed his lie-detector test. Seeing her contrite, he makes her his confidante and extracts from her a promise not to betray to Claudius his secret; namely, that he is only "mad in craft" (III, iv, 188). She solemnly assents:

> Be thou assur'd . . .
> . . . I have no life to breathe
> What thou hast said to me (III, iv, 197-199).

Similarly, in the First Quarto, the Queen at this point swears to second her son in his plan.

> Hamlet, I vow by that majesty
> That knows our thoughts and looks into our hearts,
> I will conceal, consent, and do my best
> What stratagem soe'er thou shalt devise (11, III, 4, 105-8).[11]

Gertrude keeps her promise, reporting to Claudius falsely that their son, "mad as the sea and the wind," has killed Polonius in a "lawless fit" and "'a weeps for what is done" (IV, i, 7-8, 27). Act III thus brings a complete reversal in Hamlet's opinion of his mother. He begins by proclaiming with bitter tongue, "And would it were not so, you are my mother" (III, iv, 16), but by the close he has won her collaboration. She enters into the plot with her son freely upon learning of the murder, inasmuch as she evidently had not been privy to it. He now confronts his adversary with two proved friends, the long faithful Horatio and the freshly redeemed Gertrude.

There remains the mystery of Gertrude's inability to see the specter. In Act I Horatio, Hamlet, and the Danish guards behold and recognize the spirit of their departed monarch, but in Act III the Queen never does see the Ghost of her late spouse. His appearance to his son but not to her breaks the pattern, raising the tantalizing question of why he hides his spirit form from her.[12] Unless Hamlet simply possesses more extrasensory perception than his mother, at least three answers suggest themselves. Possibly the Ghost does not wish to frighten Gertrude; perhaps the spirit fears to estrange her by manifesting himself, since this might suggest that he is suspicious of her; probably the specter does not reveal himself because he wants his son to win sole credit for redeeming her.

Hamlet's estimate of his father seems to have undergone no similar reversal. The Prince does busy himself with corroborating the Ghost's story. He tends to question its mundane authority, wondering if the spirit may not be the devil (II, ii, 628). Yet he never denies or scorns his father as he does his mother. His earlier disdain for Gertrude derives largely from his suspicion that she is partner to the crime. In this light, all of his reactions to her seem perfectly normal. In Act III he trusts her enough to confide in her fully, proposing confederation and depending on her to safeguard his disguise. Her part in the final scene of Act V confirms his reliance on her. Her cry of warning to him prevents Claudius from escaping Hamlet's filial sword of vengeance.

Hamlet's admiration for his father never deviates. This esteem, appropriate for a prince, has small basis in sentiment. The kingly father merits such respect because of his military prowess. The austere Hamlet probably never romped with his son. The young Prince's childhood male companion was the court jester Yorick: "He hath borne me on his back a thousand times" (V, i, 203-204). Prince Hamlet, then, is unprepared for intimate confidences from his father's shade, and this itself would perturb him profoundly. Unable to shake off his agitation, how can he avoid the logical consequences? Claudius would read suspicion of himself into Hamlet's agitation. In almost the first words to the Prince, the uncle reproaches him: ". . . obstinate condolement is a course/Of impious stubbornness" (I, ii, 93-94). After speaking with the Ghost, Hamlet might recall these words, for prolongation of his grief would likely arouse his uncle's suspicions. To allay these suspicions, the Prince has to discover a device to account for his perturbation and to serve his plan.

For a device, the resourceful Hamlet chooses to feign foolishness; for he confides to Horatio that he thinks it "meet/To put an antic disposition on —" (I, v, 171-172). This camouflage enables him to mask his espionage. The ruse recommends itself because of his histrionic bent. His interview with the traveling players exhibits an informed acquaintance with theatrics. He skillfully counterfeits madness, misleading everyone except the wary Claudius. His choice of a madman's part shows good judgment, and he acts it to perfection. He convinces the people of Elsinore; even the shunned "grave-maker" has heard of his condition, describing him as "he that is mad, and sent into England . . . because 'a was mad" (V, i, 163-164, 166). Apparently his mother is also taken in as he eventually has to tell her, "I essentially am not in madness" (III, iv, 187). One does not know to what cause the Danish populace attributes their scholarly Prince's behavior. As warriors, they may well have thought that the shock of his father's death, crowding upon a student whose brain has been turned by over-application to books,[13] has unsettled his reason. Or they may have regarded as a contributory factor his excessive love for Ophelia. At any rate, they do not question the genuineness of his mental aberration.

For practical reasons, then, the Prince capably resorts to madness as a masquerade. It is gratuitous to diagnose it as symptomatic of an Oedipus complex, where "Intense clinging to Oedipal wishes leads to conflict with reality, and, in order to avoid this conflict, many defense mechanisms are set up by the ego."[14] Hamlet reiterates that he adopts his course by decision, judging it "meet" to his objectives. He dons madness as a mask of trickery. It thus is not a matter of instinct or inclination to melancholy. Had it been so, a psychoanalytical interpretation could be entertained. Shakespeare nowhere intends to confuse the spectator, much less confound a recent commentator like G. Wilson Knight, who finds Hamlet an actual madman, "who must walk alone within the prison of mental death."[15]

The Oedipus theory would not have been here discussed at such length had it not been affirmatively reviewed in 1950 by Professor Lionel Trilling, who says that "There is, I think, nothing to be quarreled with in the statement that there is an Oedipus situation in *Hamlet;* and if psychoanalysis has indeed added a new point of interest to the play, that is to its credit."[16]

To have done with the psychoanalysts, one may cite a parallel in *Titus Andronicus* where Queen Tamora chooses the Moor Aaron for her lover and bears him a child. Tamora's choice appalls her two sons, who revile the Moor.

> And therein, hellish dog, thou hast undone her.
> Woe to her chance, and damn'd her loathed choice!
> (IV, ii, 77-78).[17]

Nobody has ever accused those two sons of an Oedipal attachment to their mother. Her unorthodox choice outrages them. The same sense of indignity imbues Hamlet.

Surely nothing can be gained through a psychoanalytical interpretation that cripples Hamlet with actual mental instability. The notion flatly contradicts both the precedent in Shakespeare's sources and the wily plotter's own deliberate avowal to confound his opposition by simulating silliness. One may better turn to earlier literary conventions for a more plausible parallel.

CHAPTER THREE

Hyperion to a Satyr

WHEN Hamlet raises the ancient cry of "Frailty, thy name is woman!" (I, ii, 146), he expresses agonized bewilderment at Gertrude's choice of Claudius, a "satyr," over his father, "Hyperion." In tirades like these, does Shakespeare represent the son Hamlet as psychotically oversensitive or normally reactive? What, one may reasonably ask, have the dramatist's sources to do with this question?

The phenomenon by which a woman chooses an inferior as mate, whether from feebleness of will, sensuality, or her hidden desire for power, receives hardly more than a mention in Belleforest, Shakespeare's acknowledged source.[1] In pondering the problem, one discovers that early folklore presents this phenomenon as a definite literary motif.[2] The motif recurs in some form in world literature throughout the ages and affords universal prototypes of the villainous Claudius and the heroic King Hamlet as rival suitors. Prince Hamlet's tirades thus echo the consternation of other males who have been puzzled and appalled by the unpredictability of women.

An early instance occurs in the Sanskrit collection of tales known as the *Katha Sarit Sagara*. Here a merchant's daughter "did not desire even Indra for a husband" and refused this god in favor of a common thief.[3] A similar ancient Hindu gatherum, *The Panchatantra*, includes another example in the story of a human maiden who was born a mouse. After becoming a human being, she is given the choice of the greatest elements — "mountain, sun, and cloud, and wind" — but rejects them for a male mouse. As a consequence, she is turned into a mouse again. Another tale in *The Panchatantra*, entitled "The Ungrateful Wife," concerns the spurning of a healthy man for a physical defective.[4] In it a Brahman's wife meets a cripple in the forest and falls in love with him. The cripple protests, "But what can you do with an invalid like me?"

She remains adamant: "Be still; you must make me your bride." Thereupon he does so; and she vows, "From this moment I give you my person for life."[5]

The somewhat later Oriental collection, *Tibetan Tales,* contains an expanded version of the foregoing Hindu account of the wife and the cripple. It more closely parallels Shakespeare in combining adultery with a murder theme. The Tibetan redaction, entitled "How a Woman Requites Love," tells of Prince Vísakha, who wedded a princess. He once saved her from dying of hunger when "he sliced some flesh off his hams and gave it to her to eat, and then he opened the veins of both his arms and gave her the blood to drink." The tale next records how this husband rescued a cripple from drowning and "handed him over to his wife, thanks to whose care he recovered entirely." Now, the story goes on, "it happened that Vísakha indulged only from time to time in amorous pleasure." The wife therefore "began to allure the man who had no hands or feet." At first the cripple objected that the Prince had saved and succored him "and that if he were to behave in such a way he would be putting himself into a position like unto that of a murderer." But with the evil woman continuing to tempt him "he finally acceded to her request." Desiring to do away with her husband, the adultress feigned a headache and asked him to fetch her a medicinal plant from a dangerously steep ravine. She promised to hold fast the rope for him, but her intent (later unrealized) was murder by treachery. After he began to lower himself, "she let go of the rope with her hand, whereby he also lost hold of it and fell into the water at the bottom."[6]

Greek mythology represents the theme in examples where women select mortals for their mates instead of gods. Marpessa chooses the mortal Idas over the god Apollo.[7] The superior Apollo also fares poorly with another female, Koronis, who rejects him in favor of a mere man, Ischys of Arkadia.[8] Even goddesses spurn the gods for mortals. Eos, daughter of Hyperion and Theia, marries the commoner Tithonos.[9] In another myth Selene bestows her virginity on an unworthy lover when she enters the woods with the deity Pan, a creature "with the horns, ears, and legs of a goat."[10]

Early English literature keeps the theme popular in a number of well-known pieces. In "The Thrush and the Nightingale" (ll. 115 ff.) the Thrush's antifeminism gains support from history when the bird cites the case of a noblewoman who selects a crippled man. "Think of Constantine's Queen," this bird says, "who loved a deformed beggar."[11] In the medieval romance *Sir Eglamour,* an Earl's daughter refuses emperors and kings to accept a knight for a husband.

> Yyt wylle sche not have of thoo,
> But in godenes hur holdyth so,
> The whych y trowe ys for thy love and no mo.
> Sche wolde a kynge forsake,
> And soche a sympulle knyght to take,
> But yf thy love were in hur herte wroght (ll. 76-81).[12]

The medieval *Prose Merlin* complains that females fail to appreciate a good man when they have one ("ffor woman is of that nature and of that disire, that whan she hath the moste worthi man of the worlde to hir lorde, she weneth she have the werste"); they execute "hir volunte" with evil men in "the foule corage and the foule thought that thei have. . . ."[13]

Renaissance England continues the strain of condemnation in poetry and proverb. Observing her preference for an unproved lover, one proverb asks a woman

> Canst thou be so light of love, as to change
> with every wind? So unconstant as to prefer a
> new lover to thine old friend?[14]

In the "Ballate Against Evil Women," written about 1568, the anonymous author reiterates the same old complaint: no matter how many handsome servants a lady may have, she will "tak a crippill, or a creatour/Deformit as ane owle [be] dame Natour."[15] Edmund Spenser, in a similar comment on how women favor "Lechery" (a personified character) over more handsome males, ends with the plaintive question heard through the ages:

> O who does know the bend of women's fantasy?[16]

Rather than enlarge on the point or trace the motif throughout its various ramifications, all one need observe is that Shakespeare utilizes the idea in *Titus Andronicus* and *Richard III,* continuing the tradition unbroken. In *Titus Andronicus* Aaron the Moor bewitches Tamora, Gothic queen and Empress of Rome, and fetters her "in amorous chain,/And faster bound" her to him "Than is Prometheus tied to Caucasus" (II, i, 15-17). True to the literary type of inferior man, Aaron is repulsive.

> What signifies my deadly-standing eye,
> My silence and my cloudy melancholy,
> My fleece of wooly hair that now uncurls
> Even as an adder when she doth unroll
> To do some fatal execution? (II, iii, 32-36).[17]

In *Richard III* the Duke of Gloucester, after the fashion of Claudius, murders the husband of Lady Anne and marries the widow. This inferior Duke, "Deform'd, unfinish'd," is "scarce half made up" (I, i, 20-21). He contrasts sharply with his opposite, Anne's late spouse Edward.

> A sweeter and lovelier gentleman,
> Fram'd in the prodigality of nature,
> Young, valiant, wise, and, no doubt, right royal
> (I, ii, 243-245).

Even Richard wonders at the frailty and short memory of Anne, faults which resemble those of Gertrude.

> Hath she forgot already that brave prince,
> Edward, her lord, whom I, some three monthe since,
> Stabb'd in my angry mood at Tewksbury? (I, ii, 240-242).

> And will she yet abase her eyes on me,
> That cropp'd the golden prime of this sweet prince,
> And made her widow to a woeful bed? (I, ii, 247-249).

> On me, whose all not equals Edward's moiety?
> On me, that halts and am misshapen thus? (I, ii, 250-251).

The reappearance of these traditional ideas in *Hamlet* thus occasions no surprise. The ancient theme of woman's selection of a mortal over a god, of an unworthy mate over a superior suitor, occupies a dominant role in Shakespeare's drama. It explains both the exasperation of the Ghost in *Hamlet* and the consternation of his son. Small wonder that the Prince is shocked and first cries out his hurt in flights of soliloquy. Gertrude's actions dishonor her first husband and shame her son. First, his consternation shows itself in his comparisons of the two brothers.

> My father's brother, but no more like my father
> Than I to Hercules (I, ii, 151-153).

> So excellent a king; that was, to this,
> Hyperion to a satyr (I, ii, 139-140).

> This realm dismantled was
> Of Jove himself; and now reigns here
> A very, very — pacock (III, ii, 293-295).

Of these, it is the "Hyperion" figure that echoes in his mind, as shown when he returns to it two acts later in his interview with the Queen.

> See, what a grace was seated on this brow:
> Hyperion's curls, the front of Jove himself (III, iv, 55-56).

> Could you on this fair mountain leave to feed,
> And batten on this moor? (III, iv, 66-67).

Second, Gertrude's precipitate wedding heightens his dismay.

> That it should come thus!
> But two months dead: nay, not so much, not two
> (I, ii, 137-138).

It also stirs him with a sense of doom.

> O, most wicked speed, to post
> With such dexterity to incestuous sheets!
> It is not, nor it cannot come to good (I, ii, 156-158).

In these passages, as in many another, he exhibits how his shame first drives him merely to revile himself. Perhaps he expresses self-abasement as balm to soothe his injured spirit, when he bemeans himself in successive exclamations: "O, that this too too sullied flesh" (I, ii, 129); "O all you host of heaven! O earth! What else?" (I, v, 92); and "O, what a rogue and peasant slave am I!" (II, ii, 576). If so, the balm does not last, for the Ghost will not let him be. The repeated spectral manifestations of his father keep the issue alive. The Ghost's constant ridicule of Claudius ("Ay, that incestuous . . . beast," I, v, 42) no less than his belittlement of

Gertrude agitates the Prince; it keeps the wound open, to bleed afresh with each thought of his mother's having broken her bed-vow. This is what the Ghost means when he declares that Claudius

> . . . won to his shameful lust
> The will of my most seeming-virtuous queen (I, v, 45-46).

On the grounds of this passage and the centuries-old pattern it proffers, it appears more likely than otherwise that Gertrude consorted with the "adulterate" Claudius before the death of King Hamlet.[18] In some respects she embodies the mysterious, contradictory nature of universal woman; she is one of Shakespeare's most elusive characters. In other respects she accords with the traditional examples of conscienceless females who dishonor or murder their husbands. The Elizabethan audience was familiar with tragedies of revenge and expected to see a wicked queen as in *Gorboduc*, which set the fashion.

Considerable surprise may have been built up in Act III. There the son attacks his mother's past, finally accusing her of murdering his father the late King. Her incredulous exclamation, "As kill a king!" (III, iv, 31), followed by other disavowals, convinces the son of her innocence. By introducing this unexpected element; namely, a contrite queen more weak than evil, the dramatist forsakes the conventional formula. But until her redemption at the end of this act, her moods and apparent apathy to conditions in Elsinore can hardly be construed except in terms of her wickedness.

The speed with which Claudius won Gertrude affords another justification for pursuing this assay of her motives. In the literature on the female's preference for an inferior mate, the woman usually selects a weakling because she can control him. The impression one receives of Hamlet's father is that of a strong ruler, one who in life managed the affairs of Denmark on his own. This left the Queen in those days much to her own devices. When her husband died, she may have decided to demand a larger voice in matters of state. She could hardly do this if her son became king and she simply queen-mother. This circumstance could account for her silence on her son's candidacy. Evidently she may have secured what she desired in a compact with Claudius, who early in the drama calls her "Th' imperial jointress to this warlike state" (I, ii, 9), a more potent title than queen-mother. Perhaps the Ghost alludes to such an understanding when he tells Hamlet that Claudius had plied his suit with "traitorous gifts" (I, v, 43). This phrase, no further elucidated in the text, may mean the territories of Denmark and Norway as the "gifts"; "traitorous" may refer to the usurper's offering to share their governance with Gertrude.

At any rate, woman's lust for power has already crystallized as a literary convention by the date of Shakespeare's composition of *Hamlet*. Again as before, the idea is not drawn from Belleforest. In his work Geruthe assures her son that she would "have resisted the Tyrant" and "would surely have saved the life of my Lord and husband," had it been possible.[19] In medieval England the idea of female "sovereignty" becomes the central theme of a famous group of stories in Chaucer's *Canterbury Tales*. The most celebrated of these, "The Wife of Bath's Tale," features a knight searching hard and long for the one thing women most desire. He finally encounters an old lady who yields him the answer, and he is able to tell the court that

> Wommen desiren to have sovereyntee
> As wel over hir housbond as hir love,
> And for to been in maistrie hym above (1038-1040).[20]

This reply proves satisfactory. To meet his pledge to the old woman, he marries her, making her his absolute sovereign. At the end, the Wife of Bath gives the following warning to all married men.

> . . . Jhesu Crist us sende
> Housbondes meeke, yonge, and fressh abedde,
> And grace t'overbyde hem that we wedde,
> And eek I praye Jhesu shorte hire lyves
> That wol nat be governed by hir wyves (1258-1262).[21]

The anonymous romance of the earlier Middle Ages, *Ponthus and Sidone*, bids women to wed young men because they can be ruled and will be obedient.

> Therefore, as me semes, it wer bettre to haue a yonge knight of high kynrede, that wolle abide and dwell with you, and that wold thynk himself to [be] beholden to haue worsshipp by hys wyfe; and in so myche he shuld be the more enclined to obey you and the reaume.[22]

The choice here of a young knight who "wolle abide and dwell with you" parallels Gertrude's choice of Claudius, who stayed at Elsinore, over adventurous King Hamlet, who went afield to war.

Shakespeare's acquaintance with Middle English ballads and romances was a part of his heritage as a poet. He knew some of the early authors by name; for example, the *Confessio Amantis* of the fourteenth-century John Gower figures as a source for *Pericles, Prince of Tyre.* In this play Shakespeare makes Gower the Chorus who introduces all five acts.

> To sing a song that old was sung,
> From ashes ancient Gower is come,
> Assuming man's infirmities,
> To glad your ear and please your eyes (I, 1-4).[23]

At first glance, Shakespeare in *Troilus and Cressida* appears to be less acquainted with Geoffrey Chaucer, despite the similarity of their titles. Shakespeare follows, not so much Chaucer's *Troilus and Criseyde,* as Henryson's *Testament of Cresseid;* however, since Henryson's poem is included as one of Chaucer's writings in Speght's early collection, the Elizabethan playwright would reasonably infer that Chaucer was its author. The dramatist must also have known other works by Chaucer, although he does not mention him by name. Shakespeare's poem on "The Phoenix and the Turtle" has for its most famous analogue Chaucer's "Parliament of Birds." Furthermore, in *Henry IV, Part II,* Shakespeare refers to a man named Skogan: "I see him break Skogan's head at the courtgate" (III, ii, 32-33). The worthy he most likely has in mind is Chaucer's noted friend, Henry Skogan, to whom the medieval poet addressed an "Envoy." The passage in Shakespeare's play sounds like a biographical remark by Speght in his edition of *Chaucer* in 1598.[24] To connect the plot of *Hamlet* with medieval patterns is a natural association. It is thus pertinent to note that in Chaucer's "Manciple's Tale," the wife of the God Phoebus betrays him by chambering with a mortal "lemman" (ll. 203-204, 238-239).

The medieval idea that women desire to rule also remains a significant theme throughout Renaissance literature. An ambitious queen dominates the early tragedy of *Gorboduc,* and Shakespeare himself peoples *Cymbeline, King Lear,* and *Macbeth* with a gallery of domineering princesses.[25] But one does not think of Gertrude as a wicked queen — rather as a sinner who repents and saves herself. Perhaps one should compare her with the types described in "The Naturall Disposition of Most Women," composed by Leonard Wright, a contemporary of Shakespeare.

> Most women, by nature, are sayd to be light of credit, lusty of stomake, vnpatient, full of words, apt to lye, flatter & weep; whose smiles are rather of custome then of curtesie, and their teares more of dissimulation, then of grief, all in extremes, without meane, either loving deerly, or hating deadly, desirous rather to rule, then to be ruled, despising naturally that is offered them, and halfe at death to be denied of that they demaund.[26]

Gertrude patently is not as bad as all this, although she may have been "desirous rather to rule, then to be ruled," and she appears to enjoy her new position as an influential queen. Yet, there is no body of evidence to implicate her in the murder of her husband. At all events, the Queen moves over to the side of God and right in Act IV when she joins her son in the campaign to foil the usurper. Her character therefore can be largely vindicated.

Can anything favorable be said for the character of Claudius? Recent scholarship sympathetically reexamines his part in the action. Certain authorities find him urbane and convivial, intelligent and witty, friendly at first toward his stepson and warm throughout in his regard for the Queen. They hold him to be an efficient statesman and claim that it is his diplomacy which maintains the peace. Such a view diminishes the Prince's name by exalting his opponent's. In 1918 Professor Howard Mumford Jones, with his monograph *The King in Hamlet*, became the pioneer advocate of this reading. He there commends in particular Claudius's sincere love for Gertrude. Jones reads this into both the King's triple reasons for murdering his brother ("my crown, mine own ambition, and my queen," [III, iii, 55]) and his later remark about her to Laertes.[27]

> She is so conjunctive to my life and soul,
> That, as the star moves not but in his sphere,
> I could not but by her (IV, vii, 14-16).

The defect of this interpretation is that the context of the two passages makes it clear that they mean something far different. The first passage occurs in a soliloquy where the King, overcome by the rankness of his offense, realizes that he is "still possess'd/Of those effects for which I did the murder," (III, iii, 53-54). The fact weighs heavily on his troubled mind. He does not offer his love for Gertrude as a justification of his act; he regrets the price he has had to pay for an offense that "smells to heaven" (III, iii, 36). The second passage (IV, vii, 14-16), however, is evidently only a puff by the King, serving as a trick to ingratiate himself with Laertes by appearing to be a thoughtful, loving husband. This puff comes after Gertrude lies to him about Hamlet's killing Polonius in a fit of madness. Claudius, knowing Hamlet to be sane, would realize that his wife is defending her son and would note the shift in her allegiance.[28]

Olav Lökse's corollary theory of Claudius as a kingly king[29] and expert statesman centers on four points: his presumed resourcefulness, his fine judgment in retaining Polonius from the late King as his Lord Chamberlain, his good will toward the Prince, and finally his acknowledged keen wit. This reading was in one part anticipated by the influential G. Wilson Knight, in whose *The Wheel of Fire* Claudius becomes "an excellent diplomatist and king."[30] As for this king's resourcefulness, Knight believes that "His speech to the ambassadors bears the stamp of clear and exact thought and an efficient and confident control of affairs":[31]

> . . . we here dispatch
> You, good Cornelius, and you, Voltimand,
> For bearing of this greeting to old Norway;
> Giving to you no further personal power
> To business with the king, more than the scope
> Of these delated articles allow (I, ii, 33-38).

But Knight's opinion is based on faulty reasoning because the negotiations with Norway come to naught, and in the end Fortinbras dons the crown upon the death of Claudius. Moreover, his subsequent employment of Rosencrantz and Guildenstern, first, as private investigators to unravel Hamlet's secret and, second, as hirelings to remove him from Elsinore in the sea voyage to England both end in abject failure. It likewise seems perverse to argue that King Claudius exhibits good judgment in retaining Polonius, for clearly Polonius is not an asset. His identification of the source of the Prince's madness as distracted love, while not an unreasonable assumption, fails to disclose the secret of Hamlet's pretense but alerts the Prince to the presence of spies about him. And what about the King's esteem for Hamlet? The Prince sees through the King's promise to make him the immediate heir and consequently is not dissuaded from his revenge. The King's wit, on the other hand, is genuine, but the Ghost correctly calls it "witchcraft" (I, v, 43) because it serves only the Devil's ends. The ultimate implications of Knight's theory become absurd, placing it in the same category as the old, rejected view that Hamlet, "being a very clever and wicked young man who wants to oust his innocent uncle from the throne . . . 'faked' the Ghost with this intent."[32]

What, then, is the true character of Claudius? At the beginning of the play he has attained his ambition. He now wears the Danish crown; he is completely satisfied to address his nephew as his successor to the throne. He had committed a perfect crime: there were no possible witnesses to the murder, no accessories, and no suspicion of him by any living person. How could King Claudius, or anyone else, ever surmise that the ghost of his victim would return to uncover the hideous secret? But after that secret is out, Claudius plunges from one criminal plot to another, neglecting the war with Norway to hold what he has gained and to save his own miserable life. In the first three acts Prince Hamlet busily engineers devices to wring a confession from the King, manipulating speeches of the Players and tormenting the Queen into repentance. From that point on, it is the King who even more busily spins webs of deceit against his opponent. Claudius arranges the encounter between Ophelia and Hamlet, the espionage of Rosencrantz and Guildenstern, the sea voyage to England, and the duel between Laertes and Hamlet. In this wise, the aspirant nephew and the reigning uncle equally enact the role of trickster. The tables turn as nephew and uncle alternately seek to enmesh each other. They never exchange characters: Hamlet remains on God's side; Claudius, on the Devil's.

The literal import of Shakespeare's text can not be denied. The dramatist depicts insistently a "rotten" (I, iv, 90) Elsinore headed by an unrepenting villain. From the Ghost, one learns that Claudius has committed adultery, murder, and incest. From Hamlet, one hears the further charges that the King is a lecher, carouser, and drunkard. As such, he fits neatly into the scheme of literary convention. He is Shakespeare's grand example of the inferior suitor who triumphs in love over a paragon. Shakespeare possibly toyed with the notion of an elemental contrast between brothers, King Hamlet as a god of the Sun and King Claudius as a deity of the Earth. In the First Quarto, the Prince likens Gertrude's new husband to Vulcan, Classical forger of metals within the Earth.

> Look you now: here is your husband;
> With a face like Vulcan;
> A look fit for a murder and a rape,
> A dull, dead hanging look, and a hell-bred eye,
> To affright children and amaze the world
>   (11, III, 4, 36-40).[33]

In the picture of Hyperion and a satyr, Shakespeare invents no new plot and pilfers no old page from history. The Bard follows literary and folk traditions of his own day. In writing about three of the central figures — a noble husband, his disloyal wife, and her unworthy lover — he refurbishes materials that originated in the ancient world but that are timeless in their application.

This excursion into world folklore clears up a problem that has perplexed successive generations of critics, and, more to the point, offers balm for Hamlet's wounded name. His fulsome lauds of his father's every feature ("A station like the herald Mercury" [III, iv, 58]) and his extended strictures on his mother's choice do not project an abnormal sentimentalist's disturbed mouthings. These outbursts voice in the Elizabethan mode mankind's age-old protest of woman's perverse preference for the inferior man.

CHAPTER FOUR

Blasted With Ecstasy

LOOK now at Shakespeare's reprise and reprise-with-variation illuminates another mystery in the play, throwing light on Hamlet's reasoning in his disavowal of Ophelia. Here the technique of refrain parellels that of classical music. B. H. Haggin in *Music for the Man Who Enjoys 'Hamlet'* remarks that "This effect, in music, of the return to something which has been departed from is one to take note of."[1] Nearly everything in the play happens twice or more. The Ghost appears and reappears. The Prince loses his father; Ophelia, hers. The murder plot is reproduced in the play-within-the-play. Throughout the action, Shakespeare frequently introduces a theme, draws away from it, and then repeats it exactly or with slight modification. His method is comparable to that of a symphony with "an opening statement, a departure, a return."[2]

The haunting resonance of echo enriches the Prince's diction. He constantly repeats himself: "O God! God!" (I, ii, 132); "Fie on 't! ah fie!" (I, ii, 135); "Words, words, words" (II, ii, 194); "except my life, except my life, except my life" (II, ii, 221).

On finally penetrating Hamlet's masquerade, one discovers, with no surprise, a resumption of one of the basic initial themes. This theme of woman's spurning a better man for an inferior returns in the episode of the Prince and the Lord Chamberlain's daughter. By spying on Hamlet for Polonius and Claudius, Ophelia estranges herself from her lover and aligns herself with the adversary. As Gertrude had rejected her first husband for Claudius, so now Ophelia turns against the Prince to aid this same King. The validity of this reading, which underscores and widens the application of Hamlet's point about "frailty" among women (I, ii, 146), emerges irresistibly in an objective analysis of the hero's troubled amour with Polonius's daughter. The nature of their relationship, whether illicit or otherwise, forms a part of the puzzle. By unriddling it,

one may expose the moral standards at Elsinore and gain an in-
sight into the actions of Hamlet and Ophelia. More significantly,
Hamlet's growing uneasiness over Claudius's employment of
Ophelia to pry out his secret is thrown into relief. As Hamlet
explores the evidence against his uncle, this jealousy reveals itself
as a new, personal reason for his revenge.

The first glimpses of Hamlet the lover are drawn along conventional lines. They show nothing more than a typical Elizabethan
suitor, pallid and nervous, hatless, and in dishabille. Ophelia so
delineates him to her father.

> My lord, as I was sewing in my closet,
> Lord Hamlet, with his doublet all unbrac'd,
> No hat upon his head, his stocking foul'd,
> Ungarter'd, and down-gyved to his ankle,
> Pale as his shirt, his knees knocking each other (II, i, 77-81).

She further reports that the Prince then behaved most strangely:
he remained utterly speechless throughout their meeting and
gestured enigmatically.[3]

> He took me by the wrist and held me hard;
> Then goes he to the length of all his arm,
> And, with his other hand thus o'er his brow,
> He falls to such perusal of my face
> As 'a would draw it. Long stay'd he so.
> At last, a little shaking of mine arm,
> And thrice his head thus waving up and down,
> He rais'd a sigh so piteous and profound
> That it did seem to shatter all his bulk
> And end his being; that done, he lets me go;
> And, with his head over his shoulder turn'd,
> He seem'd to find his way without his eyes,
> For out o' doors he went without their help,
> And, to the last, bended their light on me (II, i, 87-100).

Immediately Polonius recognizes these agonies as the throes
of love. This would be the stock Elizabethan diagnosis, as in Sir
Thomas Overbury's "The Amorist." In his thumbnail sketch, Overbury specifies the self-same traits.

> He is vntrvst & vnbvttoned, vngartred. . . .
> He answeres not, or not to the purpose; and
> no maruell, for he is not at home.[4]

Hamlet's dress and pantomime bespeak the apogee of love. The Lord Chamberlain expounds to Ophelia: "This is the very ecstasy of love" (II, i, 102). Ecstasy becomes the key word when she later echoes him. This "most deject and wretched" lady sees Hamlet's "unmatch'd form and feature of blown youth/Blasted with ecstasy" (III, i, 163, 167-168). His lovesickness would make a choice piece of court gossip. Both Claudius and Gertrude hear of it from Polonius. Subsequently, the Queen, who can not see the Ghost, deduces that "ecstasy" is responsible for her son's presumed hallucination.

> This is the very coinage of your brain:
> The bodiless creation ecstasy
> Is very cunning in (III, iv, 137-139).

The son is brought up short by her imperception, but it is her reference to his love-madness that prompts him to finish out this last verse with the one-word exclamation, "Ecstasy!" (III, iv, 139).

In this scene two circumstances surprise Hamlet: first, his mother does not see the apparition; second, she thinks Hamlet's love for Ophelia has driven him to hallucinations. The first he accepts as a simple fact without question; the Queen's second reaction shocks him into his exclamation. This reinforces his decision to simulate insanity and persuades him to cast himself as a lover "blasted with ecstasy" (III, i, 168). In other parts of the action Hamlet extends this dissembling to include other modes of masquerade. He masquerades before Polonius and Ophelia, before his alter ego in his self-chastising soliloquies, and before Claudius in his ostensibly naive assent to the sea voyage. In instances like these the Prince takes on the function of a stage director, one bent on plotting the moves of his unwitting victims. He also dissembles when his improvised playlet sets out to test the King, but has for final result his winning allegiance from the Queen.

Is there a true Hamlet lurking behind these masquerades? One Hamlet stalks about the stage vigorously devising cunning plots against his adversary; then another Hamlet cancels out this impression by remaining behind to indulge in false self-recriminations about inaction and apathy. Here he engages in a kind of medieval debate between desire and restraint or in a hard game against himself. Illustrating the latter, he heaps abuse on his own head and then rebuts the accusations.

> Am I a coward?
> Who calls me villain, breaks my pate across,
> Plucks off my beard and blows it in my face,
> Tweaks me by the nose, gives me the lie i' th' throat
> (II, ii, 598-601).

> Why, what an ass am I! This is most brave (II, ii, 611).

A hero like this Hamlet must be watched — nay, studied — because he epitomizes the trickster, caviling and equivocating. His motives can not be accepted at face value. A fine strand of meaning has to be drawn from the false threads he knots so confusingly to web the cunning in which he excels. One must determine, not only whether his love is real or feigned, but also why he at times makes it look like one rather than the other.

To Polonius, the Prince's lovesickness is authentic: the lover sinks into a melancholy fit because, at her father's insistence, Ophelia purposely rejects him.

> . . . I went round to work,
> And my young mistress thus I did bespeak:
> "Lord Hamlet is a prince out of thy star.
> This must not be;" and then I prescripts gave her,
> That she should lock herself from his resort,
> Admit no messengers, receive no tokens.
> Which done, she took the fruits of my advice;
> And he, repell'd, — a short tale to make —
> Fell into a sadness, then into a fast,
> Thence to a watch, thence into a weakness,
> Thence to a lightness, and, by this declension,
> Into the madness wherein now he raves,
> And all we mourn for (II, ii, 139-151).

This recountal would appeal to the court as a likely justification for both Hamlet's odd behavior and his freakish appearance. It elicits momentary credence from the suspicious, guilty King. It gains a final confirmation from the hero himself in the Grave

Scene. There Ophelia's brother Laertes leaps into her grave to enfold "her once more in mine arms" (V, i, 273). The Prince plunges in after him, declaring

> I lov'd Ophelia: forty thousand brothers
> Could not, with all their quantity of love,
> Make up my sum (V, i, 292-294).

In Act III, the protagonist Hamlet needs as many allies as he can muster. His confidence in Gertrude wins her to his side. Why, then, needing Ophelia's comfort and aid, does he not confide in her? The answer is that he believes that he cannot trust her. She occupies at court the position of an accepted member of the inner circle, where her services as an eavesdropper would be invaluable. But she has already given her trust to her father and Claudius. Hamlet, peerless dissembler, sees through her thin disguise at once. In Act III she comes to him "to re-deliver" his letters (II, i, 94). But he will not accept them, pretending that he has lost his memory: "No, not I;/I never gave you aught" (III, i, 95-96). He next questions her chastity: "Ha, ha! are you honest?" (III, i, 103), advising her to repair to a nunnery if she be innocent. Then he catches her in a white lie. He knows that Polonius stands behind the arras with the King, so he asks her, "Where's your father?" (III, i, 132). When she answers, "At home, my lord," her paltering lie confirms what he long has suspected. Her transfer of loyalty from her lover to his enemies Hamlet construes as a profound betrayal.[5] He now turns upon her with withering sarcasm.

> I have heard of your paintings, well enough. God hath given you one face, and you make yourselves another. You jig, and you amble, and you lisp and nickname God's creatures and make your wantonness your ignorance (III, i, 150-153).

To Ophelia's outraged lover the betrayal is unpardonable, and he interprets her actions as a duplicate of those of his mother in siding with Claudius.

These sentiments should not be taken as the generalizations of a university student who knows nothing except books. The Prince is a mature man, with some knowledge of the ways of women. At least he knows the prostitute's penchant for cursing and self-pity.

He compares his role with a bawd's, likening himself to a "stallion"
and soliloquizing that "I"

> Must, like a whore, unpack my heart with words,
> And fall a-cursing, like a very drab,
> A stallion! (II, ii, 614-616).

Unless he likes obscenity, which his training and character
belie, his bold interchange with Ophelia at the play-within-the-
play implies a rather marked familiarity. In their conversation,
"country matters" refers to sexual intercourse and the yonic "nothing" to the vulva.[6]

> *Ham.*   Lady, shall I lie in your lap?
> *Oph.*   No, my lord.
> *Ham.*   I mean, my head upon your lap?
> *Oph.*   Ay, my lord.
> *Ham.*   Do you think I meant country matters?
> *Oph.*   I think nothing, my lord.
> *Ham.*   That's a fair thought to lie between maid's legs.
> *Oph.*   What is, my lord?
> *Ham.*   Nothing.
> *Oph.*   You are merry, my lord (III, ii, 119-129).

Ophelia's good-natured rejoinder reflects her enjoyment of Hamlet's dalliance. Later in the same scene, the erotic references in
their dialogue are even more unmistakable.

> *Oph.*   You are keen, my lord, you are keen.
> *Ham.*   It would cost you a groaning to take off my edge.
> *Oph.*   Still better, and worse (II, ii, 258-261).

The character of their verbal interchanges adds another commentary on morals at Elsinore, where adultery, fratricide, and incest
earlier achieved a crown for the usurper Claudius.

In a recent evaluation of Ophelia, J. Dover Wilson identifies her
as a "prostitute."[7] Wilson directs attention to the Chamber Scene
with Gertrude, where the Prince accuses his mother of

> Such an act
> That blurs the grace and blush of modesty,
> Calls virtue hypocrite, *takes off the rose*
> *From the fair forehead of an innocent love*
> *And sets a blister there* (III, iv, 41-46).

According to Wilson, the lines he italicizes apply to Ophelia, the word "blister" referring to the branding of a harlot.[8] This British critic further observes that "Hamlet treats Ophelia like a prostitute; and the only possible defence for him is to show that he had grounds for so doing."[9] These grounds, Wilson claims, are established in Polonius's declaration to Claudius that "I'll loose my daughter to him" (II, ii, 162).

Still more recently, Olav Lökse, in an endorsement of this derogatory identification, finds all the references "emphasizing the element of sexual immorality which is everywhere present where Ophelia is concerned."[10] The Scandinavian scholar, along with such others as Tieck and Madariaga, thus concludes that the Chamberlain's daughter was "a bad girl."[11] But this interpretation, while supported by the prototypes of Ophelia in Saxo and Belleforest, leaves too much unexplained to warrant acceptance. Moreover, Shakespeare in these scenes notably departs from his sources in alienating Hamlet from Ophelia, for in Saxo the decoy woman moves over to his side and protects him from his enemies. Had Shakespeare's heroine been a drab, everybody in Elsinore would have known it and nobody there would have been concerned for her reputation.

Another more tenable theory proposes that Ophelia is Hamlet's mistress. First, this would explain why her treachery tents him so deeply. Second, an illicit affair with a gentlewoman would more likely remain a secret than a relationship with a prostitute. This theory would explain why Laertes does not know precisely what the relations between the lovers are and merely has doubts about the Prince's intention. As her brother, he would be among the first to hear of Ophelia's bawding. It will be remembered that Laertes warns his sister not to lose her honor "or your chaste treasure open/To his unmaster'd importunity" (I, iii, 31-32). Danish folk tradition upholds virginity as a treasure; it bears the name of "maiden crown." The advice of Laertes harmonizes with a Danish version of "Heer Halewijn," where a brother permits his sister, also named Ophelia, to go with Halewijn on the condition that she retain her virtue. Meanwhile, Hamlet's provocative words to Polonius, the cryptic Biblical allusion to "Jephthah, judge of Israel," as well as his "One fair daughter" and "a treasure" (II, ii, 422-426), betray his disquiet over her collusion with Claudius.[12]

Another passage perhaps alludes to her association with the King, for Hamlet earlier has discerned that he also is "too much in the sun" (I, ii, 67), or in the King's eye, and now he declares:

> Let her not walk i' th' sun: conception
> is a blessing, but as your daughter may conceive —
> Friend, look to 't (II, ii, 185-187).

If Ophelia had a "blister," as Wilson seems to believe, it was the King who raised it. This reasoning might gain further support from Hamlet's remark to Polonius, "you are a fishmonger" (II, ii, 173). Aware of the Lord Chamberlain's desire to improve his status, the Prince may refer to Polonius's readiness to barter his daughter in order to effect his ambition, for he is willing to degrade Ophelia in order to draw Hamlet out ("I'll loose my daughter to him," [II, ii, 162]). The oldster pretends not to understand the Prince, although the word fish has the well-known erotic connotation of "woman."[13] When the Prince calls the Chamberlain a "fishmonger" (that is, a pander), he has in mind primarily a figurative meaning deriving from ancient times, which would be current in Elizabethan England. In Hindu mythology Cupid is a fisherman who baits his hook with a woman in order to catch men.[14] To Hamlet, Polonius the fishmonger will stoop to using Ophelia as his bait.

The Prince's treatment of Ophelia has usually been judged harsh. But his rejection of her is the time-honored method of a man with a faithless maid. Hamlet's reaction to Ophelia's betrayal is instantaneous. He first advises her, if she be innocent, to "go thy ways to a nunnery" (III, i, 131-132), addressing her familiarly as "thee" and "thou" ("I'll give thee . . . be thou as chaste," [III, i, 139-140]). But when he finds her in a lie, his ardor perceptibly cools, and he changes to the formal "you"[15] in addressing her ("You jig . . . and make your wantonness your ignorance" [III, i, 151-153]). Ophelia has become the plural "you" and universal womankind. His disappointment reaches a zenith because he has gone to her for comfort. Hamlet's vain appeals to Ophelia classify him as the type of person who seeks comfort, not the sort who drowns in sorrow and sinks into a lethargy. In "A Dyalogue of Comforte Agaynste Tribulacyon," Sir Thomas More contrasts the two types sharply.

> One sorte that will seeke for no coumforte, another sorte that
> will . . . first one sorte there are, that are so drowned in sorowe,
> that they falle into a carlesse deddelye dulnesse, regarding
> nothing . . . no more then if they laye in a letarge. . . .[16]

Harsh toward Ophelia as this explanation of the Rejection Scene
may be, it yet expresses more sense than a hoary theory "that
Hamlet, being a disguised woman in love with Horatio, could
hardly help seeming unkind to Ophelia,"[17] or a new one which
accuses him of "murdering his love of Ophelia."[18] The Prince is
not "the ambassador of death walking amid life";[19] he is the
scourge and minister of God who torments his victims until they
become conscience-stricken and redeem themselves or die. Hamlet's Pyrrhus speech about "Aeneas' tale to Dido" (II, ii, 471) contains a hint that his duty to avenge his father has disrupted his
love for Ophelia.[20] Her derelictions now make it easier for him
to turn to this more important mission.

Hamlet the lover therefore blends logically into Hamlet the
avenger. His machinations result in his mother's penitence. His
actions may or may not drive Ophelia to commit suicide, for
everybody at court locates the cause in her grief over her dead
father. His plottings almost overcome the King and do bring him
to prayer (III, iii, 36-72). (In the First Quarto Claudius breaks
into tears ["O that this wet that falls upon my face" (9, III, 3, 1)]
and yearns to cleanse his soul.[21]) Seeing his uncle at prayer, the
Prince spares him, hoping to apprehend him at his more customary
dissipations.

> When he is drunk asleep, or in his rage,
> Or in th' incestuous pleasure of his bed,
> At game a-swearing, or about some act
> That has no relish of salvation in 't (III, iii, 89-92).

The hero lacks the occasion but not the inclination.

Meanwhile Hamlet as avenger makes the villain sweat. The
King's suffering and nervousness mount as the play progresses.
Claudius bends his knees in confession but arises unrepentant,
overwhelmed with the enormity of his crimes as he numbers them.
Living in constant fear of his life after his frightened exit from
"The Murder of Gonzago," he sees his countermoves come to
naught in discouraging succession. His first disappointment comes

when he realizes that the Queen, after conspiring with her son, lies about the death of Polonius to protect the killer. No longer able to trust her, Claudius in Act V conceals from her the fact that the royal cup contains poisoned wine. The failure of Ophelia to pry her lover's secret from him would cause Claudius further discomfiture. So would the paltry findings of her father that come from his interview with Hamlet. Then, to top this, his tools, Rosencrantz and Guildenstern, prove incapable; they fail to arrive at a pertinent explanation of Hamlet's behavior.

Their interrogation of Hamlet boomerangs on the two courtiers. He sees through their subterfuge; they can not unriddle his. In reply to their inquiries he makes the folk equation of north with madness and south with sanity and uses the proverb, "I know a hawk from a handsaw":

> I am but mad north-north-west: when the wind is souther-
> ly I know a hawk from a handsaw (II, ii, 396-398).

To unmask these words, one may begin by recalling that the Prince is discussing matters relating to the players who are to perform at Elsinore. Rosencrantz remarks that "an aery [a nest of hawks] of children, little eyases" (young hawks; i.e., unfledged novices) are challenging the popularity of the "common players" (II, ii, 354-355, 366). It also is possible that "handsaw," a common tool, links with "Your hands" and also with "common players." However this may be, one point is clear: Hamlet is suspicious of Rosencrantz and Guildenstern. He recognizes that they are spies, because in an aside he says, "I have an eye of you" (II, ii, 301-302). It accordingly seems natural to associate Guildenstern with the well-known figurative meaning of a hawk; namely, a person who preys or spies upon another.

But what, then, does "handsaw" signify? One may reply by observing that as Hamlet is speaking, Polonius enters and launches into one of his wordy discourses. The Chamberlain becomes as echolalic as a handsaw. After hearing Polonius speak, the Prince exclaims, "Buzz, buzz!" (II, ii, 412). Hamlet clearly seeks to astonish his inquisitors. In stating that he is not wholly insane but that he can differentiate between a hawk and a handsaw, Prince Hamlet would appear to suggest that he is not as stupid as his interrogators seem to believe, that when their subterfuges are so baldly plain, he at least can distinguish between two spying courtiers and an old man as full of "buzzes" as a *handsaw*.[22] As hero, he once again exemplifies the Nordic dissembler: the Loki described by historians as *"astucieux"* (crafty), the Loki who wielded *"langage équivoque."*[23]

Uncertainty and frustration intensify the King's pain when his two spies report to him afterward the failure of their mission. Claudius questions them complainingly.

> And can you, by no drift of conference,
> Get from him why he puts on this confusion,
> Grating so harshly all his days of quiet
> With turbulent and dangerous lunacy? (III, i, 1-4).

A little later Polonius unintentionally strikes terror into the heart of the King:

> 'T is too much prov'd — that with devotion's visage
> And pious action we do sugar o'er
> The devil himself (III, i, 47-49).

Claudius, realizing that it is he who is the Devil, exclaims in an aside, "O, 't is too true!" His tribulation enjoys no respite, as one dismaying event follows hard on the heels of another. When he receives the news of the death of Polonius at the hands of Hamlet, he becomes thoroughly frightened. He tries to convince the Queen that her son is a grave menace.

> It had been so with us, had we been there.
> His liberty is full of threats to all,
> To you yourself, to us, to every one (IV, i, 13-15).

In this manner the murderer pays for his crime bit by bit in a prolonged agony of fearful apprehension. A quick death for him would be more merciful, but Hamlet wants to draw out his suffering and make him quake with fear.

The avenger of Acts IV and V is hardly the same person as the Hamlet who converses earlier with Horatio. In a long speech in Act I, Hamlet discourses with calmness, resolution, and objectivity on three kinds of faults which may damn a man in the general censure. He unveils the flaws in the innate nature of particular individuals which give them a disposition towards wickedness. His classic statement does not specify Claudius but employs the plural "men" to emphasize its larger application.

> So oft it chances in particular men,
> That for some vicious mole of nature in them,
> As, in their birth — wherein they are not guilty,
> Since nature cannot choose his origin —
> By the o'ergrowth of some complexion
> Oft breaking down the pales and forts of reason,
> Or by some habit that too much o'er-leavens
> The form of plausive manners, that these men,
> Carrying, I say, the stamp of one defect,
> Being nature's livery or fortune's star,—
> His virtues else — be they as pure as grace,
> As infinite as man may undergo —
> Shall in the general censure take corruption
> From that particular fault (I, iv, 23-36).

Here Hamlet lists, first, a defect at birth, which man can not prevent but which nevertheless prejudices others against him. Second, he names the habit that violates accepted standards of good manners; for example, the Danish habit of excessive drinking.[24] Third, he mentions the predominance ("o'ergrowth") of some physical humor — as, say, anger or melancholy — which may drive a person to murder or insanity. How completely different are the vivid comparisons in Act III, where the Prince turns from objective generalizations to subjective particulars. He borrows his figures from animals associated with witches and wizards, contemptuously reviling his uncle as a toad, a bat, a tom-cat ("a paddock, . . . a bat, a gib" [III, iv, 190]).

As the play progresses, Hamlet's choler rises, making him more dangerous. Now he shows, as Polonius earlier fears, signs of actual ecstasy,

> Whose violent property fordoes itself
> And leads the will to desperate undertakings
> As oft as any passion under heaven
> That does afflict our natures (II, i, 103-106).

In other words, all of the intensity of his passion for Ophelia, lacking now an object for its expression, transforms itself into love's opposite, hatred, and centers on the King. Hamlet's extensive investigations, even the play-within-the-play, glean no incriminating new evidence against the murderer. Something else happens in the lapse of time. The Prince unearths a second motive for his revenge in what he believes to be the disloyalty of Ophelia.

The hero, sometimes censured for unwarranted generalizations, bases his conclusions on solid grounds, on the recurrence of what he considers to be meaningful instances. His mother rejected his father; Ophelia, in his opinion, has turned against him; therefore all women are faithless. It matters not to the argument if Ophelia be innocent of any wrongdoing;[25] he believes her guilty. When Hamlet places her defection in the same category as his mother's disloyalty to his father, the theme of woman's spurning the better choice rings out in reprise.

The derelictions of Polonius and especially those of his quondam friends Rosencrantz and Guildenstern likewise leave a mark on Hamlet. Musing on grievances, he now broadens his thesis into a condemnation, not of woman alone, but of all mankind: the world is an "unweeded garden" (I, ii, 135); "The time is out of joint" (I, v, 189); and the age is "drossy" (V, ii, 197). Hamlet, a civilized university student, has at last molded himself into a justified avenger, with a cynical outlook on life and ample motive for revenge. The repetition of misfortune brings about the transformation. As in the Biblical analogy, he has turned his face to his attacker and has been struck on both cheeks (Luke, 6:29). For the Prince there now can be no abatement of the pressure on Claudius. He drives the King to dismay when in major scenes of the play Hamlet matches him move for move, never permitting himself to be outwitted. For a man whom the court regards as a crazed lover, the erstwhile melancholy Dane has been metamorphosed into an avenger bold and alert. He now knows this character to be his true self, knows that he has to challenge Claudius openly. Hamlet must now accomplish his revenge forthrightly and lay aside his mask of ecstasy.

CHAPTER FIVE

Points of Mighty Opposites

BY Act IV the once suave Claudius has become a desperate, nervous man. All his clever ruses have come to naught. Hamlet has utterly outwitted him on the terra firma of Denmark. The King thereupon proposes to vanquish his enemy on the sea. The striking shift in setting, namely from land to sea, points up the recurrence of opposites in the denouement. Now, Shakespeare's use of reprise explains, as already suggested, such perplexing matters as the inferior-suitor theme and the Prince's rejection of Ophelia. It also explains, as will be shown, the riddle of Hamlet himself. This riddle may be solved by tracing the patterns of opposites that pervade the play.

Earlier incidents in *Hamlet* show Shakespeare at work on a major scheme of opposites when he introduces scene after scene presenting a reversal of situation. The play is in blank verse; the playlet, in rhymed couplets. Hamlet's madness is feigned; Ophelia's, real. Hamlet sees the Ghost; Gertrude does not. The Prince defers avenging the death of King Hamlet; Laertes plans straightway to avenge that of Polonius. Hamlet slays Rosencrantz and Guildenstern instead of being delivered by them to be slain. He declares he will utilize the playlet to catch the King but refuses to stab Claudius upon finding him at prayer. Neither does he probe the conscience of his uncle, but he upbraids and shames his mother. He exclaims in Act I, "I" will "sweep to my revenge" (I, v, 31) but not until Act V does he kill Claudius.

Moreover, the dominant atmosphere of contrast also suffuses the two basic themes of the central plot. The King's crime is not simply murder but fratricide, an act opposed to the laws of nature. The Queen's choice of Claudius over the elder Hamlet is not simply adultery but the unnatural preference for a baser man. Further, the element of rhetorical contrast itself has not escaped the notice of critics. In 1765 Samuel Johnson saw in the successive scenes alternating solemnity and merriment,[1] and in 1961 Horst Oppel contrasted the King's comforting the Prince in his loss with his goading Laertes to avenge Polonius.[2] Finally, the omnipresence in *Hamlet* of the oxymoron, or contradictory epithet, underscores the important place of opposites in Shakespeare's pattern. Their ultimate effect, as they pile relentlessly one upon another, is to overwhelm the audience with a profusion of contradictions. The oxymorons, like the unnatural central situation, contribute much to the final impression of a topsy-turvy world. They begin to move in that direction early in the play.

> fair and warlike form (I, i, 47).
> defeated joy (I, ii, 10).
>
> With mirth in funeral and with dirge in marriage,
> In equal scale weighing delight and dole,— (I, ii, 12-13).
>
> dearest foe (I, ii, 182).
> pious bawds (I, iii, 130).
> traitorous gifts (I, v, 43).
> Doubt truth to be a liar (II, ii, 118).
> plentiful lack of wit (II, ii, 202).
> Happy in that we are not overhappy (II, ii, 232).
> crafty madness (III, i, 8).
> Grief joys, joy grieves (III, ii, 209).
> Frost . . . doth burn (III, iv, 87).
>
> I must be cruel, only to be kind.
> Thus bad begins and worse remains behind
>   (III, iv, 178-179).

The foregoing array of opposites comprises an illustration of the Law of Polarity. The mystic Law was propounded by the legendary Egyptian philosopher, Hermes Trismegistus, who saw dark shading into light and the end into the beginning.[3] His basic principles, having a firm place in the Elizabethan mind, were commonplaces to Shakespeare. As recently suggested, the application of the Law of Polarity to the enigmatic Sonnets helps to unriddle paradoxes of black is fair and fair, black.[4] Moreover, Shakespeare's great patron, Henry Wriotheseley, Third Earl of Southampton, to whom "Venus and Adonis" (1593) and "The Rape of Lucrece"

(1594) are dedicated, was a Hermetic. Southampton had blazoned upon his coat of arms the French motto, "*Ung par tout, et tout par ung,*" which had originated as a major proposition of Trismegistus.[5] The idea of Polarity was especially persistent, reappearing in the so-called Enigma of Empedocles, where life is death and death, life. It finds its most influential expression in Plato's *Phaedo* as Socrates's Law of Opposites: the noble generates from the disgraceful and the better from the worse.[6] Chaucer's "Lack of Steadfastness," picturing the world upside down, notes the application of the formula to wilful kings. Their greedy ambitions are

> . . . so fals and deceivable
> That word and deed, as in conclusion,
> Ben nothing lyk, for turned-up-so-doun
> Is al this world for mede and willfulnesse,
> That al is lost for lak of stedfastnesse (3-7).[7]

Something quite like this occurs in the world which inverts itself in *Hamlet*. At the opening Claudius, having already won the Danish election, enjoys both his queen and his crown, and suavely dominates the negotiations with rival Norway. As the action progresses, the tables turn, and the King disintegrates. Growing uneasy, he vainly seeks to establish a family claim with mother and son as his respective "jointress" and designated heir. Soon he senses more and more "the great love the general gender" have for Hamlet (IV, vii, 18), loses the allegiance of Gertrude to his nephew, and through his neglect and ineptness allows Fortinbras to rally support in Norway and Poland. This raises the question of whether it is really the Prince who procrastinates or the King. Had Claudius removed Hamlet from Elsinore by permitting him to return to Wittenberg as the Prince at first desires, or had the uncle seen to it that Hamlet was immediately slain, the King might have retained all his gains. Instead, he conducts a losing game of matching wits with a protagonist of superior intellect. The suspicious sovereign's plan of using Polonius as an eavesdropper fails, as does his scheme for having the Chamberlain spy on the Prince. Besides, whatever advantage he may hope to gain by enlisting Ophelia as a spy is never achieved. Hamlet's jealousy in construing her actions as a betrayal actually gives him further justification for pursuing the Ghost's revenge.

Of course Claudius, already guilty of one murder, would hesitate to risk assassinating the Prince. Such an act would invite unremitting investigation. To avoid this and yet rid himself of a growing menace, he has to maneuver his nephew out of Denmark, as far away as he can conveniently send him. Pretending to protect him from the Chamberlain's avengers, Claudius has a pretext for sending him to England. That far country will thus serve as the setting for his second murder. By now the calm confidence with which the ruthless King had stolen the crown has generated its opposite — desperation.

As a wily man of parts, the Danish prince seems to sense that his uncle's desperate proposal to send him to England involves a plot to murder him. Hamlet informs his mother that he will be hard with Rosencrantz and Guildenstern.

> But I will delve one yard below their mines,
>
> And blow them at the moon. O, 't is most sweet,
>
> When in one line two crafts directly meet (III, iv, 208-219).

The "two crafts" (ships and schemes) may denote the beleaguered Hamlet's later convenient rescue by the pirates and this crafty hero's outwitting Claudius with a scheme that has the courtiers slain in his stead.[8] Since the courtiers are themselves innocent of murderous intent, the Prince's responsibility for their deaths has been held to be out of character. Yet his resort to murder conforms exactly with the Scandinavian archetype which a blood-spilling Odin, for one, illustrates. Such violence should not come as a surprise. One is prepared for it by the tenor of Hamlet's sharp asides when Claudius addresses him, and by the flavor of his pungent double-entendres in contrast to the King's transparent flattery. The Danish Prince's *langage équivoque* has renowned literary antecedents in Loki the *astucieux* and in the Icelandic saga hero, Gunnlaug the Snake-tongued, lord of astringent speech.[9]

The ingratiating early addresses of uncle to nephew, each the other's contending opposite, meet with no success. In Act I Claudius condoles with "my cousin Hamlet, and my son,—" (I, ii, 64), pretending that " 'T is sweet and commendable in your nature, Hamlet,/To give these mourning duties to your father" (I, ii, 87-88). He later invites the mourner to "think of us/As of a father"

(I, ii, 107-108). But the Prince remains impervious to such cloying expressions, remarking in an aside, "A little more than kin, and less than kind!" (I, ii, 65). Later on, he continues as perceptive as before, detecting every ruse against him and every subterfuge of Claudius's spies each time they strive to search out Hamlet's secret. He emerges from the encounters as more than a match for the King's pawns. In confounding them, he overcomes the advance guard, moving always nearer to the castle to depose the man wrongly enthroned.

This interpretation is essential to a proper understanding of the drama. In Scandinavian legend Loki possesses "cunning, wit, and skill."[10] In English letters Beowulf is the hero of brawn; Hamlet, of brain. Accordingly, the King's plot to embark him for England does not dupe Hamlet. The plan, desperate and hurried, has no depth to it. Since the King has denied his request to return to Wittenberg, the Prince naturally would suspect this reversal of the first decision. Hamlet's ingenuity in eluding the toils of his opponent derives more from crafty cogitation than from supernormal divination.

The hero of the first Acts transforms himself into his opposite in the closing ones. At first he comes upon the stage pale from cloistered study, meditative, given to introspection in the soliloquies that match Polonius for verbosity. At the end he is weatherbeaten from the sea, dueling confidently with Laertes, resolved that Denmark shall have a sovereign worthy of its destiny. It is significant that only in Act V does Hamlet forego his ubiquitous soliloquies. Their absence points up the transformation wrought in the Prince. In the denouement he catches fire and becomes the personification of boldness. Suffering grief and consternation in the first scenes, he behaves like a helpless hypnotized spectator of a chamber of horrors. He can vent his true feelings about the murder only in asides. In Act IV the real Hamlet drops his antic character forever when he writes fearlessly to the usurper:

> High and Mighty, You shall know I am set naked on your kingdom. To-morrow shall I beg leave to see your kingly eyes, when I shall, first asking your pardon, thereunto recount the occasion of my sudden and more strange return.
>
> (IV, vii, 44-48).

Shakespeare evidently intends to set in vivid contrast the earlier Hamlet and the later. To depict a protagonist as a superman throughout destroys dramatic suspense and impedes artistic character development. At first the Prince, thinking the Ghost a devil, laments "my weakness and my melancholy" (II, ii, 630). Later, convinced of his uncle's guilt, he rages:

> . . . now could I drink hot blood,
> And do such bitter business as the day
> Would quake to look on (III, ii, 408-410).

In this wise the dramatist builds his protagonist to heroic stature. Hamlet had felt substantial misgivings on his return to Elsinore from Wittenberg but feels none whatever on his second return to Elsinore after his rescue by the pirates. In terms of artistry, there is fine dramatic propriety in his transformation. Evolution of a dramatic character from weaker to stronger appeals to everyone.

This idea of a new Hamlet, a changed man, follows an earlier precedent in Shakespeare's works. In the two parts of *Henry IV* and in *Henry V* the royal Hal evolves from frivolous prince, consort of topers and drabs, and close companion of Falstaff, into a serious monarch, the successful suitor of a French princess, and the splendid victor at Agincourt. To illustrate, in the *First Part of Henry IV* Hal permits his companion to impersonate the King, whereupon Falstaff glows in familiarity.

> That thou art my son I have partly thy mother's word, partly my own opinion, but chiefly a villanous trick of thine eye and a foolish hanging of thy nether lip that doth warrant me. If then thou be son to me, here lies the point: why, being son to me, art thou so pointed at? (II, iv, 441-448).[11]

In the *Second Part* Prince Hal, cognizant of his new responsibilities, disowns the fat old rascal in the celebrated Rejection Scene.

> I know thee not, old man. Fall to thy prayers (V, v, 51).

> Presume not that I am the thing I was;
> For God doth know (so shall the world perceive)
> That I have turn'd away my former self (V, v, 60-62).[12]

In *Henry V* Hal displays no tendency to revert to his former self. Endearing himself to his English followers as a valiant soldier and an accomplished diplomat, he attains truly heroic proportions as an ideal English king.

In a similar transformation, the pensive Hamlet of Act I evolves into his opposite, the driving fury of Act V. As this nemesis, Hamlet possesses qualities of leadership rivaling those of Henry V. The Dane combines the virtues of scholar, soldier, and statesman. His scholarship makes him a master of bombast, repartee, and satire. He has a soldier's fellowship with the guards at Elsinore, a familiarity with military phraseology, some acquaintance with ships and pirates, and considerable skill with the sword. As for Hamlet's ability to inspire allegiance, Claudius attests to his popularity with the masses ("He's lov'd of the distracted multitude" [IV, iii, 4]) and Laertes warns Ophelia of his likely observance of royal precedents in his choice of a wife (I, iii, 22-24). To Ophelia, the Prince owns in addition the qualities of a courtier.

> The courtier's, soldier's, scholar's, eye, tongue, sword;
> Th' expectancy and rose of the fair state,
> The glass of fashion and the mould of form,
> The observ'd of all observers . . . (III, i, 159-162).

Hamlet's letter to her adds the datum that he could compose a passable love lyric.

> "Doubt thou the stars are fire,
>   Doubt that the sun doth move,
> Doubt truth to be a liar,
>   But never doubt I love" (II, ii, 116-119).

This last attribute sets the intellectual Danish Prince apart from the hearty English Hal. It harmonizes with the conventions of Scandinavian saga. Gunnlaug the Snake-tongued speaks in satirical verses to his enemies and in eulogistic lyrics to his betrothed.[13] Thus nature endowed Hamlet with all the sterling attributes of an exemplary monarch. It remains for Fortinbras, an outsider, to sum up his merits.

> Let four captains
> Bear Hamlet, like a soldier, to the stage,
> For he was likely, had he been put on,
> To have prov'd most royal . . . (V, ii, 406-409).

Upon what grounds does Fortinbras base his high opinion? Hamlet's reputation would be common knowledge to the Norseman, who has a vital interest in the court at Elsinore. The Norse leaders know that the Prince commands the respect of the Danish elite military circle ("As you are friends, scholars, and soldiers" [I, v, 141]) and that he owns their loyalty. In Act I he trusts Horatio, Marcellus, and Bernardo not to speak of his interview with the Ghost ("Let it be tenable in your silence still:" [I, ii, 248]). They loyally vow to protect him ("Our duty to your honor" [I, ii, 253]). Like the Saxon king as ring-giver, he straightway assures them of reward ("I will requite your loves" [I, ii, 248]). Laertes describes him to Ophelia as a noble who respects the prescripts of protocol.

> He may not, as unvalued persons do,
> Carve for himself, for on his choice depends
> The safety and health of this whole state;
> And therefore must his choice be circumscrib'd
> Unto the voice and yielding of that body
> Whereof he is the head (I, iii, 19-24).

Beyond this, the Prince embodies strong personal qualities to recommend him. He expresses unusual courage ("I do not set my life at a pin's fee" [I, iv, 65]) and firm religious conviction ("And for my soul, what can it do to that,/Being a thing immortal as itself?" [I, iv, 66-67]). Though a philosopher, he is physically strong, of solid[14] flesh, and an expert duelist. He illustrates the Nordic ideal, for in medieval times Scandinavians everywhere approved the warlike precedent of Odin as the model for a man's character. When aggrieved, Hamlet aggressively responds.

> My fate cries out,
> And makes each petty artery in this body
> As hardy as the Nemean lion's nerve (I, iv, 81-83).

The possessor of so many heroic qualities, Hamlet would be justified in considering himself worthy to be king.

Nor does the Danish prince lack aspirations. Rosencrantz intimates that "ambition" makes Hamlet stigmatize Denmark as "a prison" (II, ii, 249). The Prince admits to Ophelia, "I am very proud, revengeful, ambitious" (III, i, 125-126). In a second exchange with Rosencrantz, he broadly hints at the source of his disappointment.

> *Ham.*   Sir, I lack advancement.
> *Ros.*   How can that be, when you have the voice of the King himself for your succession in Denmark?
> *Ham.*   Ay, but "While the grass grows" — the proverb is something musty (III, ii, 354-359).

The remainder of the proverb applies fittingly to Hamlet the "stallion," since it reads, "the horse starves."[15] Finally, he discloses the font of his grievance when he states that Claudius "Popp'd in between th' election and my hopes" (V, ii, 65). The so-called elective monarchy of Denmark should not be confused with a modern elective office. The word election means "choice" (Latin *electio*). There was no peremptory reason why Hamlet should not have been chosen instead of Claudius.[16] He had moral and legal claims to the throne, since hereditary rights were then held valid.[17] This is established by the fact that the uncle of Fortinbras is still alive when in Act V the nephew becomes the "choice."

As to why so virtuous a hero takes no overt action at once, there are a dozen theories. He does not slay the King at once because he is squeamish about bloodshed; is ill; fears for his life; disbelieves in personal vengeance; has an "Oedipus complex"; thinks revenge will serve no useful purpose; resents the call to duty; wants to shield Gertrude; hopes to make sure the crown passes to the right man; desires to justify his plan; suffers from a philosophical mind that inhibits action; or seeks an auspicious moment for the deed.[18] Each of these theories reflects the complexity of Shakespeare's play, since each explores separate hypotheses and follows separate clues. Out of this welter of opinion, is it possible to advance any one explanation as totally acceptable? In undertaking to formulate such an explanation, one must bring Shakespeare's rhetorical scheme into focus. Comprising innuendoes, half-statements, and words unsaid but to be inferred, the dramatist's involved rhetoric makes meaning difficult to pin down.

It is in the culmination of contrast and counterpoint that the play yields up its secret. The aura of ambiguity disappears when one sees *Hamlet* for what it is, a balancing feat by the master

juggler of meanings within meanings. For the scheme of opposites
in the structure is harmoniously matched by a system of opposites
in the style.

This proposition presents Hamlet as an avenger superb enough
to gratify the most Italianate Englishman. Shakespeare's contemporary audiences would identify the Danish Prince as an injured
aristocrat confronted with the proud duty of avenging the dishonor to his family. According to the historian Jacob Burckhardt,
"This personal need of vengeance felt by the cultivated and highly
placed Italian, resting on the solid basis of an analogous popular
custom, naturally displays itself under a thousand different aspects
and received the unqualified approval of public opinion."[19] Burckhardt adds that "in the case of those injuries and insults for which
justice offered no redress . . . each man is free to take the law into
his own hands."[20] The indispensable specification of the Italian
Renaissance was that "there must be an art in the vengeance."[21]
Shakespeare's spectators similarly relished vengeance that was
artistic. It had to comprise material injury and moral humiliation
visited upon the offender. A "mere brutal, clumsy triumph of
force"[22] would not satisfy the playwright's sophisticated spectators, who willingly endured the lapse of time necessary for a full
revenge. In accord with the code of *bella vendetta,*[23] the Prince
has to exercise the utmost patience.

His waiting game allows one to enjoy to the limit the spectacle
of a villain writhing in fear. As avenger incarnate, he exacts meet
revenge. He requites this villain; he requites this villain's tools,
Rosencrantz, Guildenstern, and Laertes; and he requites, supreme-
ly, the Danish electorate who enthroned Claudius.

> But I do prophesy th' election lights
> On Fortinbras; he has my dying voice.
> So tell him . . . (V, ii, 366-368).

At the same time, Hamlet the Dane is no conscienceless, blood-
thirsty fury. An excess of retributory zeal drives him to abandon
his native ingenuity and trickery for his antagonist's speciality,
brute force. Resorting to such force, he effects the murder of Rosencrantz and Guildenstern, and he feels no sting of conscience.[24]
Instead, he exhibits a stern exultation:

> They are not near my conscience; their defeat
> Does by their own insinuation grow:
> 'T is dangerous when the baser nature comes
> Between the pass and fell incensed points
> Of mighty opposites (V, ii, 58-62).

The hero's tragic flaw, recourse to violence, reduces him at this juncture to Claudius's level. The transformed Prince of the Duel Scene exemplifies the gory bent of such Scandinavian prototypes as the pagan Odin, Loki, and Gunnlaug the Snake-tongued. The play does not recount the saga of a "muddy-mettled" princekin unequal to the duty of avenging family honor.

Shakespeare's most famous tragedy relates the plots and counterplots in the course of which a wily victim of injustice divests his heart of sorrow to invest it with vengeance. The wry wit-snapper ends by waking to violence; the tristful thinker ends by unsheathing a wrathful sword; the loyal Dane ends by invoking a rival Norseman as Danish king. One can at last perceive the logic of Hamlet's evolving from his inner world to the external world of Elsinore.

References

Standard abbreviations used here are *PMLA* (*Publications of the Modern Language Association*), *SAB* (*Shakespeare Association Bulletin*), and *SQ* (*Shakespeare Quarterly*).

INTRODUCTION

1. Olive Henneberger, " 'Report Me and My Cause Aright'. . .," *English Studies in Africa* (1959), II, 48-58. See also Robert M. Smith, "Current Fashions in *Hamlet* Criticism," *SAB* (1949), XXIV, 13-32. For further references, see Anton A. Raven, *A Hamlet Bibliography and Reference Guide* (Chicago, 1936); Gordon R. Smith, *A Classified Shakespeare Bibliography, 1936-1958* (University Park, Penn., 1963); and the annual bibliographies in *PMLA, Shakespeare Jahrbuch,* and *SQ.*

2. "Ophelia's Lies," *SAB* (1941), XVI, 215.

3. "Hamlet the Actor," *South Atlantic Quarterly* (1948), XLVII, 527.

4. *The Court and the Castle* (New Haven, Conn., 1957), pp. 14, 74-75.

5. In the Introduction to Karl Werder, *The Heart of Hamlet's Mystery* (New York, 1907), p. 1.

6. "Hamlet and Ophelia," *Philological Quarterly* (1956), XXXV, 393. Charlton M. Lewis conjectures that inconsistencies in the play come from Shakespeare's having written various scenes at different times (*The Genesis of Hamlet* [New York, 1907], pp. 20-21, 33).

7. W. P. Johnston, *The Prototype of Hamlet and Other Shakespearean Problems* (New York, 1890), p. 96. There are some critics who maintain in dissent that the hero proceeds as quickly as circumstances in the play allow (C. S. Lewis, "Hamlet: The Prince or the Poem?" in the collection edited by Claire Sacks and Edgar Whan, *Hamlet, Enter Critic* [New York, 1960], p. 171). But this view misinterprets the playwright's intent. For example, two of the incidents arising in the drama, the arrival of the traveling players and the King's importing of two spies, are not introduced in any sense to impede the action and thus to justify Hamlet's delay. Instead, these scenes are designed to display how the alert Prince adeptly seizes on adverse incidents to further his own plans: he employs the playlet to stir his mother to remorse and the interviews with Rosencrantz to provoke his uncle to fear and doubt. Claudius's two contrivances to save himself by killing his nephew, namely the sea voyage and finally the duel, are also episodes fashioned to exhibit Hamlet's mental agility in diverting these counterplots to his own committed course.

As the embodiment of Nordic nimbleness, he scuffles with Laertes and gains
possession of the poisoned sword, and, though mortally wounded himself, he
by a twist of Fate foils both plot and plotter.

8. "Hamlet's Hallucination," *Modern Language Review* (1917), XII, 419.

9. *Nature in Shakespearian Tragedy* (New York, 1962), pp. 25, 45. Historical interpretations hardly call for rebuttal since they do not assail the
Prince's character. Two well-known books that associate him with either
Essex or Shakespeare himself as the autobiographical original are Lilian
Winstanely, *Hamlet and the Scottish Succession* (New York, 1921), p. 10,
and A. L. Rowse, *William Shakespeare, A Biography* (New York, 1963),
p. 321.

10. Other examples of Shakespeare's acquaintance with folklore and medi-
eval literature are discussed in such works as T. F. Thiselton Dyer, *The Folk-
Lore of Shakespeare* (New York, 1883), p. 184; William Montgomerie, "Folk
Play and Ritual in *Hamlet*," *Folk-Lore* (1956), LXVII, 214-227; Frank A.
Patterson, "Shakespeare and the Medieval Lyric," *Shakespearian Studies*
(New York, 1916), pp. 431-432; Willard Farnham, *The Medieval Heritage
of Elizabethan Tragedy* (Berkeley, Calif., 1936), p. 40; and Ernest H. Cox,
"Another Medieval Convention in Shakespeare," *SAB* (1941), XVI, 249-253.

11. Though the subject is not discussed, he is so designated by Lora and
Abraham Heller, "Hamlet's Parents: The Dynamic Formulation of a Tragedy,"
American Imago (1960), XVII, 419.

12. The trickster is a familiar figure in Nordic lore (Anna B. Rooth, *Loki
in Scandinavian Mythology* [Lund, Sweden, 1961]).

13. "O God, Horatio," is possibly the most satisfactory reading (Winifred
M. T. Nowottny, "The Application of Textual Theory to Hamlet's Dying
Words," *Modern Language Review* [1957], LII, 161). On the potential re-
ligious meaning here, see Curtis B. Watson, *Shakespeare and the Renaissance
Concept of Honor* (Princeton, N. J., 1960), pp. 282-284; Roland M. Frye,
Shakespeare and Christian Doctrine (Princeton, N. J., 1963), p. 135.

CHAPTER ONE

1. *"Hamlet": An Historical and Comparative Study* (Minneapolis, Minn.,
1919), p. 25. Thomas Sheridan, as reported by James Boswell (London
Journal [6 April 1763]), made "the first detailed statement of the theory that
Hamlet was an irresolute, overthoughtful prince, shrinking from action" (J.
Yoklavich, "Hamlet in Shammy Shoes," *SQ* [1952], III, 209). The Prince
procrastinates because his world is dead (Harold R. Hutcheson's "Hamlet's
Delay," *Shakespeare Newsletter* [October, 1951], I, 19), and he does so
partly because Claudius is "a heavily guarded monarch" (Robert R. Reed, Jr.,
"Hamlet, the Pseudo-Procrastinator," *SQ* [1958], IX, 177-186).

2. "Hamlet and His Problems," *Selected Essays: 1917-1932* (New York,
1932), p. 145.

3. The screen version, produced and directed by Olivier, had its world

premiere in London during May, 1948 (John Ashworth, "Olivier, Freud, and Hamlet," *Atlantic* [May, 1949], CLXXXIII, 30).

4. *The Wheel of Fire* (London, 1949), p. 42.

5. Unless otherwise noted, all quotations from the plays are from Thomas Marc Parrott (ed.), *Shakespeare, Twenty-Three Plays and the Sonnets* (New York, 1953).

6. The drama opens about two months after the death of King Hamlet and less than one month (I, ii, 138-153) after his funeral (John E. Hankins, *The Character of Hamlet and Other Essays* [Chapel Hill, N. C., 1941], p. 12). Hamlet and Ophelia's respective dates of "two hours" and "twice two months" (III, ii, 135-136) are both false; they illustrate the pattern of opposites discussed in Chapter Five.

7. A story illustrating these points comes from the *Anglo-Saxon Chronicle* (A.D. 755), translated by the Rev. James Ingram (New York, 1938), pp. 50-51. In this story Cynehard surprises and kills King Cynewulf, whose thegns refuse Cynehard's offers and die "fighting their dead lord's murderer." Cynehard also tries to bargain for their acceptance of himself as king, but they refuse to acknowledge him (Eric John, "English Feudalism and the Structure of Anglo-Saxon Society," *Bulletin of the John Rylands Library* [1963], XLVI, 26). The guards at Elsinore would be obliged by the chivalric code to discover the identity of the murderer, track him down, and kill him. The artist Shakespeare may exclude them from reappearance after Act I in order not to violate the bonds of feudalistic vassalage and to leave the son free to avenge the crime alone.

8. According to Horatio, "Our last king . . ./Did slay this Fortinbras" (I, i, 80, 86).

9. The family feud is a favorite theme in heroic sagas; see the Ingeld episode (ll. 2032-2069) in Fr. Klaeber's edition of *Beowulf* (Boston, 1928), pp. 76-77. Moreover, in this Old English epic the fire drake guards a treasure; in this connection, Horatio asks the Ghost if he has appeared because "thou hast uphoarded in thy life/ Extorted treasure in the womb of earth" (I, i, 136-137). A medieval atmosphere saturates *Hamlet*. Claudius's fratricide illustrates the disintegration of the bonds of kinship, which N. K. Sidhanta notes as a characteristic of the early epic (*The Heroic Age of India* [New York, 1930], p. 116, n. 1).

10. The play does not identify the species of snake involved.

11. Coleridge regards the conversation opening the drama as unimportant talk about the weather (Thomas M. Raysor [ed.], *Samuel Taylor Coleridge, Shakespearean Criticism* [New York, 1962], II, 225).

12. Hamlet and Horatio are interested in silencing Marcellus so that he will not reveal what he knows about the Ghost or possibly suspects about Claudius (Olav Lökse, *Outrageous Fortune* [New York, 1960], pp. 24-25).

13. Claudius may have used a poison that would render the corpse repulsive to the sight in order to destroy the image of the late King as a military hero. Evidently Hamlet's father died a painful death. If he made an outcry, either nobody heard him or the murderer bribed the guards to ignore his

screams. As for the name of the poison, Sir John Charles Bucknill suggests hebenon, which is "capable of producing leprosy" (*The Medical Knowledge of Shakespeare* [London, 1860], p. 260); Frank Sullivan, hydrargyrum ("Hamlet's Hebona and Mercury Poisoning," *Los Angeles Tidings* [December 31, 1948], p. 9); David I. Macht, aconite, which has "a blood coagulating effect" ("A Physiological and Pharmacological Appreciation of *Hamlet*," *Bulletin of the History of Medicine* [1949], XXIII, 193); and R. R. Simpson, henbane (*Shakespeare and Medicine* [Edinburgh, 1959], p. 137). According to A. L. Rowse, Shakespeare's "hebona" comes from Marlowe's *The Jew of Malta* (*William Shakespeare, A Biography* [New York, 1963], p. 326).

14. Stomach does not mean courage or resolution but refers to a secret purpose of the Norsemen, which is vengeance on Denmark (Vlas Kozhevnikov, ". . . Some Enterprise that Hath a Stomach in 't . . .," *SQ* [1961], XII, 71-72). As for the specter, Robert H. West asserts that one does not know the Ghost's religious denomination and can not determine it ("King Hamlet's Ambiguous Ghost," *PMLA* [1955], LXX, 1117). Hamlet momentarily entertains the idea that the Ghost may be an evil spirit, and in that era a prominent traditional superstition held that the melancholy man was an easy victim for the Devil (Lawrence Babb, *Elizabethan Malady* [East Lansing, Mich., 1951], p. 108).

15. Richard Flatter believes that the Ghost knows that Gertrude is guilty of murder but conceals this fact from their son (*Hamlet's Father* [New Haven, Conn., 1949], p. 62). Flatter also asserts that the Ghost remains invisible to Gertrude "because she has murdered him" (*ibid.*, p. 77).

16. For a reprint of the English translation of 1608, see Cyrus Hoy (ed.), *Hamlet* (New York, 1963), pp. 131 ff.; for its French original, see François de Belle-forest Comingeois, *Le Cinquiesme Tome des Histoires Tragiques* (Paris, 1572), fols. 149 r. ff.

17. According to ancient Hebrew custom, a man was expected to marry his brother's widow, especially if she were left childless (Genesis, 38:8 and Deuteronomy, 25:7). Shakespeare's plot is not a parallel, for Claudius murdered his brother and married a widow with a son. Simon A. Blackmore holds their marriage invalid because the King did not secure the required dispensation to wed his deceased brother's wife (*The Riddles of Hamlet and the Newest Answers* [Boston, 1917], p. 46).

18. In early legendry Amleth, whose name means "mad Ole," is the rightful heir (Kemp Malone, *The Literary History of Hamlet* [Heidelberg, 1923], pp. 52, 267).

19. Oliver Elton (tr.), *The Nine Books of Saxo Grammaticus* (London, 1905), I, 221. On the earliest record of the name in England, see Rev. L. G. Hunt, *The Munsley Stone, The Ancient Tombstone Inscription now deciphered as "Hamlet Xhethi" Prince of Denmark, The "Hamlet" of Shakespeare. Dated 362 A.D.* (Ledbury, Hereford, 1926), pp. 1-12.

20. Scandinavian folklore features a trickster in Loki, the Satan of Norse mythology, "the contriver of all fraud and mischief" (Thomas Bulfinch, *Bulfinch's Mythology* [New York, 1913], p. 332).

21. Shakespeare's contemporary, Gabriel Harvey, classifies the play as a revenge tragedy; as such, he judges that it will "please the wiser sort" (Albert B. Weiner [ed.], *Hamlet, The First Quarto* [Great Neck, N. Y., 1962], p. 6). As is well known, the play develops a revenge theme similar to that in Thomas Kyd's *The Spanish Tragedy*. The present study contends that the revenge motive and Hamlet's trickery outweigh the problem of Hamlet's delay.

CHAPTER TWO

1. A. A. Brill (tr.), *The Basic Writings of Sigmund Freud* (New York, 1938), p. 310.

2. "Hamlet and the Psychologists," *Shakespeare Newsletter* (April, 1963), XIII, 20. For another example of this type of interpretation, see Arthur Wormhoudt, *Hamlet's Mouse Trap: A Psychoanalytical Study of the Drama* (New York, 1956).

3. Ernest Jones, *Hamlet and Oedipus* (New York, 1949), p. 59.

4. Noel Coward, *Play Parade* (New York, 1933), pp. 425-498; Hyman Plutzik, *Apples from Shinar* (Middletown, Conn., 1950), p. 49; Hope H. Moulton ridicules the subject in introducing the Prince as tied to his mother's "apron strings" (*Hamlet, A Burlesque in One Act* [Boston, 1927], p. 1).

5. *Dark Legend* (New York, 1949), p. 222.

6. Theodore Reik, "In My Mind's Eye, Horatio," *Complex* (1952), VII, 15-31; Norman Symons, "The Graveyard Scene in *Hamlet*," *International Journal of Psycho-Analysis* (1928), IX, 96-119; and Ernest Jones, "The Death of Hamlet's Father," *International Journal of Psycho-Analysis* (1948), XXIX, 174-176.

7. James C. Maloney and Laurence Rockelein, "A New Interpretation of Hamlet," *International Journal of Psycho-Analysis* (1949), XXX, 98-109.

8. This irony does not exist for its own sake: rather it forms part of Shakespeare's satirization of the melancholy man as a stock character of Elizabethan theatre. Others include Antonio in the *Merchant of Venice*, Jaques in *As You Like It*, and especially Malvolio in *Twelfth Night*.

9. Genesis, 38:8 and Deuteronomy, 25:7. On adultery as meaning incest or any misuse of the sexual powers, see Bertram Joseph, *Conscience and the King, A Study of Hamlet* (London, 1953), p. 17. *Cf.* Note 17 below.

10. This is the conjecture of Richard Flatter, *Hamlet's Father* (New Haven, Conn., 1949), pp. 64 ff. But the Queen may have reasoned far differently. Had she been privy to the murder or learned of it from her new husband, she might have preserved silence to protect her son from possible assassination in case he attempted to slay Claudius. She nonetheless remains interested in her new husband's welfare to the last, for when Laertes cries out bitterly to him about the murder of Polonius, Gertrude absolves Claudius of guilt ("But not by him" [V, v, 128]). Carolyn Heilbrun argues convincingly that the Queen was not a party to the late King's murder but unconvincingly that the Ghost's word "adulterate" does not "necessarily mean that he believed Gertrude to

have been false to him before his death" ("Character of Hamlet's Mother,"
SQ [1957], VIII, 201, 206). According to Lora and Abraham Heller, the
specter remains invisible to Gertrude because she has committed adultery
("Hamlet's Parents: The Dynamic Formulation of a Tragedy," *American
Imago* [1960], XVII, 416). Whatever her degree of guilt, her consternation
on hearing Hamlet's accusation is either remorse or genuine innocence. On
this account, the Ghost evidently wants to help his son to redeem her:

> But look, amazement on thy mother sits.
> O, step between her and her fighting soul (III, iv, 112-113).

11. Albert B. Weiner (ed.), *Hamlet, The First Quarto* (Great Neck, N. Y.,
1962), pp. 138-139. Although he does not construe the whole improvised play
as a test of Gertrude's guilt or innocence, Robert M. Smith perceives that "The
speeches of the Player Queen are carefully contrived for this purpose"
("Hamlet and Gertrude, or The Conscience of the Queen," *SAB* [1936], XI,
88). Pearl Hogrefe correctly reads the scene between Hamlet and his mother
(III, iv) as the turning point of the drama ("Artistic Unity in *Hamlet*," *Studies
in Philology* [1949], XLVI, 184-195). Hamlet's mother later keeps her bargain
with the Prince (Rosamund Putzel, "Queen Gertrude's Crime," *Renaissance
Papers* [1961], p. 46).

12. Flatter, *op. cit.* W. W. Greg believes that the specter which Hamlet
sees is hallucinatory ("Hamlet's Hallucination," *Modern Language Review*
[1917], XII, 418-419). The fact that the Prince sees the specter whereas his
mother does not illustrates the scheme of opposites discussed in Chapter Five.

13. On the theory that the Prince can not "make up his mind because of
the over-reflective habit fostered at Wittenberg," see Peter Alexander, *Hamlet,
Father and Son* (Oxford, 1955), p. 88.

14. Morton Levitt (ed.), *Readings in Psychoanalytic Psychology* (New
York, 1959), p. 165. The phenomenon on display is Hamlet's skill at trickery,
which has been misread as mere histrionics (Andrew J. Green, "The Cunning
of the Scene," *SQ* [1953], IV, 398; C. R. Forker, "Shakespeare's Theatrical
Symbolism and Its Function in *Hamlet*," *SQ* [1963], XIV, 219). A subject
of the endless commentaries on the Prince is the matter of his sanity, but
Elder Olson wisely observes that in the play itself "every dramatic device is
used to establish Hamlet's sanity, and none to throw doubt on it" ("Hamlet
and the Hermeneutics of Drama," *Modern Philology* [1964], LXI, 237).

15. *The Wheel of Fire* (London, 1949), p. 21.

16. *The Liberal Imagination* (New York, 1950), p. 48.

17. G. L. Kittredge (ed.), *The Complete Works of Shakespeare* (Boston,
1936), p. 993. In a forthcoming paper in *English Language Notes*, Professor
A. S. Cairncross suggests that Gertrude was faithful to King Hamlet but that
her profound grief over her loss acted as a sexual stimulus in drawing her to
his murderer. But in Belleforest the Queen is unmistakably an adulteress, as
indeed in Shakespeare she is inferentially. Her infidelity to King Hamlet in
life explains the Ghost's reproaches, Hamlet's revulsion, her own remorse, and
so on.

CHAPTER THREE

1. Belleforest merely remarks in passing that the new King "murthered a farre more honester and better man than himself in massacring" the Prince's father (for the English translation of 1608, see Cyrus Hoy [ed.], *Hamlet* [New York, 1963], p. 137; for its French original, see *Le Cinquiesme Tome des Histoires Tragiques* [Paris, 1572], fol. 159 v.).

2. The theme of woman deserting her husband for an unworthy lover is number T 232 in Stith Thompson, *Motif-Index of Folk-Literature* (Bloomington, Indiana, 1935), V, 278. See also Kemp Malone, "Rose and Cyprus," *PMLA* (1928), XLIII, 397-446, esp. 418-419. On relating the idea to *Hamlet*, see Haldeen Braddy, "Shakespeare and Three Oriental Tales," *Midwest Folklore* (1951), I, 91-92.

3. C. H. Tawney (tr.) and N. M. Penzer (ed.), *The Ocean of Story* (London, 1927), VII, 35.

4. Arthur W. Ryder (tr.), *The Panchatantra* (Chicago, 1925), p. 357.

5. *Ibid.*, p.406.

6. F. Anton von Schiefner, W. R. S. Ralston (trs.), and C. A. F. Rhys Davids (ed.), *Tibetan Tales* (New York, n.d.), pp. 291-293.

7. H. J. Rose, *A Handbook of Greek Mythology* (London, 1953), p. 142.

8. *Ibid.*, p. 139.

9. *Ibid.*, p. 35.

10. *Ibid.*, pp. 34, 168.

11. Carleton Brown (ed.), *English Lyrics of the XIIIth Century* (Oxford, 1932), p. 105, ll. 115 ff. For remarks on the verses, see F. L. Utley, *The Crooked Rib* (Columbus, Ohio, 1944), pp. 238-239.

12. James O. Halliwell (ed.), *Thornton Romances* (London, 1844), p. 124. For remarks on the verses, see Margaret A. Gist, *Love and War in the Middle English Romances* (Philadelphia, 1947), p. 70.

13. Henry B. Wheatley (ed.), *Merlin, or The Early History of King Arthur* (London, 1869), Part III, p. 433.

14. Morris P. Tilley cites a number of instances of this idea in *Euphues* under No. 704 in his *Elizabethan Proverb Lore in Lyly's Euphues and in Pettie's Pallace with Parallels from Shakespeare* (New York, 1926), p. 335.

15. John Small (ed.), *The Poems of William Dunbar* (Edinburgh, 1893), II, 266; Utley, *op. cit.*, p. 246.

16. For *The Faerie Queene* (I, iv, 24), see J. C. Smith and E. de Selincourt (eds.), *The Poetical Works of Edmund Spenser* (London, 1924), p. 21; for remarks on Spenser, see Carroll Camden, *The Elizabethan Woman* (New York, 1953), p. 28.

17. G. L. Kittredge (ed.), *The Complete Works of Shakespeare* (Boston, 1936).

18. John W. Draper believes her innocent of adultery in *The Hamlet of Shakespeare's Audience* (Durham, N. C., 1938), p. 117.

19. Hoy, *op. cit.*, p. 140; Belleforest, *op. cit.*, fol. 162 v.

20. F. N. Robinson (ed.), *The Works of Geoffrey Chaucer* (Boston, 1957), p. 86.

21. *Ibid.*, p. 88.

22. Frank Jewett Mather, "King Ponthus and the Fair Sidone," *PMLA* (1897), XII, 142.

23. William J. Rolfe (ed.), *Pericles* (New York, 1911), p. 41. Gower also appears twice between the scenes and once in the epilogue, making a total of eight appearances. Moreover, Shakespeare seems to rely on the *Confessio* in his interpretation of the hero and to adopt the name Philoten from Gower's Philotenne (G. A. Barker, "Themes and Variations in Shakespeare's *Pericles*," *English Studies* [1963], XLIV, 410).

24. Thomas Speght, *The Workes of our Antient and Lerned English Poet, Geffrey Chaucer* (London, 1598), fol. 196 r.; Hyder E. Rollins, "The Troilus-Cressida Story from Chaucer to Shakespeare," *PMLA* (1917), XXXII, 383-429); and Thomas H. McNeal, "*Henry IV, Parts I and II*, and Speght's Edition of *Geffrey Chaucer*," *SAB* (1946), XXI, 87-93. Materials of likely ultimate Chaucerian origin also appear in *A Midsummer Night's Dream* and *The Winter's Tale*.

25. Thomas H. McNeal, "Shakespeare's Cruel Queens," *The Huntington Library Quarterly* (1958), XXII, 41-50.

26. *A Display of Duty* (London, 1616), fol. 18 v.

27. *The King in Hamlet* (Austin, Texas, 1918), pp. 47, 51, 59-97. Claudius has all the main traits of a Machiavel, but adherents of Jones's views include J. M. Beatty, Jr., who finds the uncle to be the Prince's "worthy adversary" ("The King in *Hamlet*," *SAB* [1936], XI, 239). Dr. Max Huhner objects to Beatty's reasoning and persuasively maintains that Claudius belongs in the same class as Shakespeare's other hardened criminals who wax remorseful ("Communication," *SAB* [1937], XII, 130).

28. Claudius significantly refuses to confide in the Queen thereafter and so conceals from her in Act V the fact that the cup is poisoned.

29. Professor Lökse says that kings "were to some extent above the moral law" (*Outrageous Fortune* [New York, 1960], pp. 76-77).

30. *The Wheel of Fire* (London, 1949), p. 33.

31. *Ibid.*

32. A. C. Bradley, *Shakespearean Tragedy* (London, 1926), p. 92.

33. Albert B. Weiner (ed.), *Hamlet, The First Quarto* (Great Neck, N. Y., 1962), p. 136. E. E. Stoll holds that Q1 is the dramatist's first revision (*Art and Artifice in Shakespeare* [New York, 1934], p. 90); A. S. Cairncross regards it as "a report of a cut version of Q2" (*The Problem of Hamlet* [London, 1936], p. 35).

CHAPTER FOUR

1. *Music for the Man Who Enjoys 'Hamlet'* (New York, 1945), p. 22. The musical connection one here proposes derives support from other analogies to

music in the play observed by E. E. Stoll (*Art and Artifice in Shakespeare* [New York, 1934], pp. 128, 130).

2. *Ibid.,* p. 42.

3. Hamlet interprets Ophelia's silence as corroboration of his jealous thoughts. Weston Babcock adds that "The waving of the head up and down three times is a universal gesture of confirmation" (*Hamlet, A Tragedy of Errors* [Lafayette, Ind., 1961], p. 63). In brothel usage, one may add, the gesture of going the length of the arm is an invitation to fornicate.

4. *New and Choise Characters* (London, 1615), p. 256. The Folger Shakespeare Library has a microfilm copy of the 1614 text, which is the same, from the Henry E. Huntington Library.

5. John A. Clair suggests that Hamlet's "Well, well, well" indicates his awareness of the presence of both Polonius and Claudius ("Shakespeare's *Hamlet*, III, i, 92," *Explicator* [1955], XIV, item 5); but W. Edward Farrison, who believes Ophelia guilty of relations with the King, counters with the proposal that Hamlet "suspects the presence of only Claudius behind the arras" ("Ophelia's Reply Concerning Her Father," *College Language Association Journal* [Morgan State College, Baltimore, 1958], I, 56-57).

6. Thomas Pyles, "Ophelia's 'Nothing,' " *Modern Language Notes* (1949), LXIV, 322-323.

7. *What Happens in Hamlet* (Cambridge, England, 1956), p. 103.

8. *Ibid.,* p. 101.

9. *Ibid.,* p. 103.

10. *Outrageous Fortune* (New York, 1960), p. 62.

11. *Ibid.,* pp. 45-46; Ludwig Tieck, *Kritische Schriften* (Leipzig, 1852), III, 261-264; and Salvador de Madariaga, *On Hamlet* (London, 1948), pp. 43, 65. Emphasizing Ophelia's song-bawdy fancies, Jean B. Jofen contends that she is basically immoral ("Two Mad Heroines," *Literature and Psychology* [1961], XI, 70-77).

12. On the Prince's meaning, see Arthur Johnston, "The Player's Speech in *Hamlet*," *SQ* (1962), XIII, 21-22; on the Danish materials, see Holgar A. Nygard, *The Ballad of "Heer Halewijn," Its Forms and Variations in Western Europe* (Knoxville, Tenn., 1958), pp. 43-44; R. C. A. Prior, *Ancient Danish Ballads* (London, 1860), I, xxxix.

13. Eric Partridge glosses *fish* as a prostitute and sees a sexual meaning in *fishmonger* (*Shakespeare's Bawdy* [New York, 1948], p. 113). On *fish* as a current underworld synonym for pimp, see Haldeen Braddy, "Narcotic Argot Along the Mexican Border," *American Speech* (1955), XXX, 87.

14. In the Hindu *Century of Love* the Indian Cupid is a fisherman, "who, casting on the ocean of this world a hook called woman, catches men as fishes . . . and bakes them in the fire of love" (Arthur A. Macdonell, *History of Sanskrit Literature* [New York, 1900], p. 341). Howard L. McCord compares this description with Dylan Thomas's "Ballad of the Long-Legged Bait" ("Dylan Thomas and Bhartrihari," *Notes and Queries* [March, 1961], p. 110). Ophelia would be the figurative fishhook employed in the effort

to catch Hamlet. On a trickster who gets caught on a literal fishhook (no. J 2136.2), see Stith Thompson, *Motif-Index of Folk-Literature* (Bloomington, Ind., 1934), IV, 198. To this day a man who marries is said to be *hooked*. The word *hooker* is also a synonym for prostitute.

15. G. R. Elliott comments briefly on the change from personal "thou" to impersonal "you." He conjectures that "nunnery" refers in the Elizabethan sense to a house of ill fame and that "monsters" mean cuckolds (III, i, 141, 143), (*Scourge and Minister* [Durham, N. C., 1951], p. 83 and n. 9); but E. E. Stoll argues that "nunnery" does not mean brothel ("A Spanish Hamlet," *Modern Philology* [1949], XLVII, 16).

16. *Utopia; with The Dialogue of Comfort* (New York, 1910), p. 134.

17. A. C. Bradley, *Shakespearean Tregady* (London, 1926), p. 92.

18. G. Wilson Knight, *The Wheel of Fire* (London, 1949), p. 38.

19. *Ibid.*, p. 32. By contrast, Claudius is, Knight says, "a good and gentle king" (*ibid.*, p. 35).

20. Johnston, *op. cit.*, p. 22.

21. Albert B. Weiner (ed.), *Hamlet, The First Quarto* (Great Neck, N. Y., 1962), p. 132.

22. Haldeen Braddy, "I Know a Hawk from a Handsaw," *SAB* (1941), XVI, 29-32. Hawk may mean literally a mortar board. Philip Drew reads "Hernesewe" (heronshaw) for "handsaw" ("Hawks and Handsaws," *SQ* [1960], XI, 495). As for the literal sense of "Buzz, buzz!" (II, i, 412), Hardin Craig notes in his edition that the expression is, "according to Blackstone, an interjection used at Oxford to denote stale news" (*Shakespeare* [New York, 1931], p. 756).

23. C. F. Allen, *Histoire de Danemark* (Copenhagen, 1878), I, 12.

24. In the Prince's complaint about "my weakness and my melancholy" (II, ii, 630), some critics see "a confession of Hamlet's own weakness" for drink (Lökse, *op. cit.*, p. 18). Raymond D. Thomas does not so interpret him in *Shakespeare's Alcoholics* (White Plains, N. Y., 1949), pp. 1-16. Perhaps Hamlet's "weakness" refers to his momentary physical reaction upon hearing that his father had been murdered. The Prince already suspects it, for he exclaims "O my prophetic soul!" (I, v, 40). In Icelandic sagas and the person of Merlin-Lailoken, madmen are clairvoyant and prophetic (Enid Welsford, *The Fool* [New York, 1936], pp. 105, 112).

25. Ophelia's speeches sometimes appear capable of more than one meaning; at least her admonition to her brother to heed his own advice (I, iii, 51) may be either pure innocence or arch deception. Perhaps her mask is innocence just as Hamlet's is madness. See further Note 11 above. According to J. Mark Patrick, Shakespeare commits himself to no single interpretation of Ophelia ("The Problem of Ophelia," *Studies in Shakespeare* [Coral Gables, Fla., 1953], p. 144). Patrick nonetheless says that she may have been pregnant by Hamlet and that his refusal to marry her may have driven her to suicide (*ibid.*, pp. 140-141); but this proposition has been rather thoroughly scouted by S. A. Tannenbaum, "Mistress Ophelia," *SAB* (1939), XIV, 252.

CHAPTER FIVE

1. *The Plays of William Shakespeare* (London, 1765), VIII, 311.

2. "Kontrast und Kontrapunkt in Shakespeare-Drama," *Shakespeare Jahrbuch* (1961), XCVII, 153-182. "A part of Hamlet's experience, over the play, is to pass from one of these extreme positions to the other: from centrality to isolation" (John Holloway, *The Story of the Night* [Lincoln, Neb., 1961], p. 26). Another design in the play is to contrast war and peace (Paul A. Jorgensen, *Shakespeare's Military World* [Berkeley, Calif., 1956], p. 207). Even the Prince's friends are contrasted: Horatio is faithful; Ophelia, faithless (Leo Kirschbaum, "Hamlet and Ophelia," *Philological Quarterly* [1956], XXXV, 389). Major opposites develop, it may be added, between Hamlet's caustic language and Osric's affected speech; between Ophelia's doing away with herself and Hamlet's merely thinking of suicide; between the Ghost's exhortation that his son destroy Claudius and the Ghost's reservation that he spare Gertrude; and so on.

3. *The Kybalion* (Chicago, 1908), p. 154.

4. Haldeen Braddy, "Shakespeare's Sonnet Plan and the Effect of Folk Belief," *Midwest Folklore* (1962), XII, 235-240.

5. T. W. Baldwin, *On the Literary Genetics of Shakespeare's Poems & Sonnets* (Urbana, Ill., 1950), p. 175.

6. For Empedocles, see John Burnet, *Early Greek Philosophy* (London, 1930), p. 245; for Plato, see Harold N. Fowler (ed.), *Euthyphro, Apology, Crito, Phaedo, Phaedrus* (London, 1926), I, 245.

7. F. N. Robinson (ed.), *The Works of Geoffrey Chaucer* (Boston, 1957), p. 537.

8. "Crafts" means literally ships and figuratively schemes. On the further idea that Hamlet cleverly uses instruments wrested from his adversaries to overcome them, see Warren V. Shepard, "Hoisting the Enginer with his own Petar," *SQ* (1956), VII, 281, 284. One may observe that the Prince's ability to turn the tables on his opponents exhibits an order of supertrickery.

9. C. F. Allen, *Histoire de Danemark* (Copenhagen, 1878), I, 12; and Margaret Schlauch (tr.), *Medieval Narrative, A Book of Translations* (New York, 1934), pp. 35-72.

10. Thomas Bulfinch, *Bulfinch's Mythology* (New York, 1913), p. 332.

11. G. L. Kittredge (ed.), *The Complete Works of Shakespeare* (Boston, 1936), p. 560.

12. *Ibid.*, p.620.

13. Schlauch, *op. cit.*

14. In Elizabethan times "solid" would be pronounced "sullied." Shakespeare evidently intends a play on pronunciation, so that the spelling of the word is immaterial. The reading "sallied" makes little sense. J. Dover Wilson favors "sullied" (*The Manuscript of Shakespeare's "Hamlet" and the Problems of Its Transmission* [Cambridge, England, 1934], II, 307-315). "Solid," however, matches with the picture of the Prince as both "fat" and "thirty," against

which E. E. Stoll unpersuasively remonstrates ("Not Fat or Thirty," *SQ* [1951], II, 295-301). A youthful thirty, which may echo *Dr. Faustus* (XIV, 24), is strongly reasserted by James J. McKenzie ("Hamlet's Age Again," *Notes and Queries* [1956], n. s. III, 151-152). Shakespeare achieves verisimilitude in depicting the Danish Prince as brawny. In early Denmark "personal courage and physical strength, united with clear judgment, were necessary to win distinction" (George P. Hansen, *The Legend of Hamlet* [Chicago, 1887], p. 11).

15. "Stallion" appears a better word than the variant "scullion." A "stallion" is a male habitué of brothels, the opposite of a female habituée, or "drab" (II, ii, 614-616).

16. John E. Hankins, *The Character of Hamlet and Other Essays* (Chapel Hill, N. C., 1941), pp. 95-97. Claudius formally names Hamlet his successor (I, ii, 109), so that the Prince has the right to name Fortinbras or anybody else as his own successor. The monarch's word carried weight but was not always decisive. Hamlet's father would have naturally designated his son, not his brother, had the "election" been normal.

17. Besides having a moral and legal claim to the throne, Hamlet has a command from God to punish his uncle because the Ghost proves to be a good spirit (Sister Miriam Joseph, "*Hamlet*, A Christian Tragedy," *Studies in Philology* [1962], LIX, 119-140; but see Paul N. Siegel, "Discerning the Ghost in *Hamlet*," *PMLA* [1963], LXXVIII, 148-149).

18. Alfred Harbage, *As They Liked It* (New York, 1961), pp. 97-100.

19. S. G. C. Middlemore (tr.), *The Civilization of the Renaissance in Italy* (New York, 1945), p. 267.

20. *Ibid.*

21. *Ibid.*

22. *Ibid.*

23. *Ibid.*, p. 268. Hamlet properly achieves his ends alone, telling the sympathetic Horatio, "Let be" (V, iii, 235).

24. Although most critics regard the two courtiers as innocent, W. W. Lawrence states that there is "nothing which establishes conclusively either the innocence or the guilt of Rosencrantz and Guildenstern" ("Hamlet's Sea Voyage," *PMLA* [1944], LIX, 59). T. M. Parrott dissents from this view, believing that Hamlet is taken prisoner by the pirates and then ransomed ("Hamlet's Sea-Voyage — Bandits or Pirates?" *SAB* [1944], XIX, 51-59). It appears that the Prince has, as a part of his purpose, to wreak vengeance upon both Claudius and his tools, so that it is inaccurate to maintain "that Hamlet dies in our eyes a lesser man" (Thomas Greene, "The Postures of Hamlet," *SQ* [1960], XI, 365). Whatever his faults, the Prince in his reliance on Providence undergoes at the end a spiritual rebirth (S. F. Johnson, "The Regeneration of Hamlet," *SQ* [1952], III, 206-207). Yet the spiritual rebirth ascribed to Hamlet seems subordinate to his final transformation. In Act V the transformation into bloody nemesis forms a mighty opposite to the earlier Hamlet the cogitator, whose meditations in one soliloquy even touch upon his own suicide (III, i, 60-82).

NOTE ON THE AUTHOR

HALDEEN BRADDY, a native East Texan, joined the faculty of Texas Western College in September, 1946. He earned his doctorate at the age of twenty-six under the eminent medievalist Carleton Brown at New York University in February, 1934. Dr. Braddy then studied in England and France through a grant from the American Council of Learned Societies in the summer of 1937. For the past thirty years, he has published more than a hundred scholarly articles, principally in the fields of Chaucer, folklore, language, and Shakespeare. Some of these have appeared in both the *Shakespeare Association Bulletin* and its successor, the *Shakespeare Quarterly*. The author has taught college English since 1929 and has been active in the American Folklore Society and the Modern Language Association.